WHAT OTHERS ARE SAYING . . .

Wow! You truly made pedagogy day a highlight of our conference. People were so excited by your ideas and the energy was palpable. I was so impressed by all the time you took to attend so many events, including on day one. I was amazed at your opening address, it was so tightly organized, you got so many of your salient points in, it was funny, easy to follow, with an entertaining powerpoint. It was such a pleasure experiencing your work again. It was fun and inspirational to see you in action. A HUGE Thank You! - **Dr. Barbara Fast, Chair of Piano Pedagogy, University of Oklahoma**

Thank you for your inspirational presence at the recent GP3 Forum at the University of Oklahoma. Your keynote presentation; "Coaching for Performance: Helping Pianists Get Out What is in Them," was thoroughly engaging and just what we pianists needed, in the words of many participants. In short, you were stellar! - **Dr. Lisa J. Zdechlik, Associate Professor of Piano Pedagogy, University of Arizona**

"This journal strengthened the mental components of my practice and performance, with incredible results. I feel more in control and at ease in my performance, allowing each performance to be an enjoyable experience." - **Dr. Rebekah Jordan-Miller, Assistant Professor of Piano, Shorter College**

Because of your book my last recital was a new experience for me. I found myself engaged and enjoying my performance, and even being spontaneous at times. Your concentration tools made the world of difference for me. I was often able to get my focus back easily when it drifted without jarring myself into errors or panic. I wrote performance scripts, and made a schedule of my recital day. Thanks for all your efforts and sharing your ideas and wisdom with us musicians! - **Dr. Sara Ernst, New School for Music Study, Kingston, NJ**

I feel like I really know what to do when it comes to mental preparation for a recital. I never realized that Tiger Woods and Mozart could have so much in common! You bring energy and enthusiasm to each new challenge, and your passion and curiosity have inspired me to take my performances to the next level.- **Elaina Burns, Doctoral student, University of Oklahoma**

We were so glad to have you come and speak to us. You gave us a lot of ideas to think about and to put into practice. You did an amazing job! It was great to meet you and we wish you all the best.- **Wendy Green, Central Oklahoma Music Teachers Association**

You were absolutely a HIT! All the teachers and performers were thrilled with what you had to say, the manner in which you presented, and your very personable style. Thank you again for a fabulous, engaging, enlightening seminar. Everyone was so enthusiastic about you and what you had to say. I woke up thinking about the seminar and can't wait to start employing some of your ideas in my practicing for my concert next weekend. Everyone seems to be reeling from all the information you presented. As I said before, you were a wonderful, engaging speaker, with so much to say. I hope that I can bring you back to Chicago sometime, sooner rather than later.- **Heidi Mayer, President, Chicago Area Music Teachers Association**

I found your seminar to be intrinsically important and feel that all of your principles should unquestionably be a part of every music performance curriculum. While I was getting ready for my performance, I mentally reviewed some of my notes from the seminar and mentally scripted my performance. Taking everything you said today into account, I ended up having one of the best performances I've had in a long time and feeling great both before and after! - **Diego-Alonso, Spanish Guitar, Chicago, Il**

PLAYING YOUR BEST
○ ○ ○ ○ ○ ○ ○ ○ ○
WHEN IT COUNTS

Mental Skills for Musicians

Dr. Bill Moore

Moore Performance Consulting Publications
Norman, Oklahoma

Published by Moore Performance Consulting
2011 Trail Pine Ct.
Norman, OK 73070

Orders@www.playingyourbest.com
Contact@bill@playingyourbest.com

All rights reserved. No part of this publication may be reproduced, stored in a retrieval system, or transmitted in any form or by any means, electronic, mechanical, photocopying, recording and/or otherwise without prior permission of Bill Moore.

Copyright 2010 Bill Moore
ISBN-13 978-0-9792873-2-9
ISBN-10 0-9792873-2-4

www.playingyourbest.com

Special thanks to:

Nicki, my wife and best friend, who has kept me green and growing despite my kicking and screaming.

The Boys (Brennan, Tyler, Cullen and Ian). You guys are the best ensemble I could ever ask for.
I love you all.

Jane Magrath, my true stage mother who has championed my talents, as well as inspired, pushed and challenged me throughout this project.

Barbara Fast for getting all this music stuff started.

All my graduate students over the years who helped make this book better!

And,
My parents, Bill and Glee Moore who taught me there is a light at the end of every tunnel.

Contents

INTRODUCTION: *Parallel Paths To Excellence*   1

CHAPTER 1: *Harnessing Your Passion To Perform*   9

CHAPTER 2: *Mental Skills For Musicians*   31

CHAPTER 3: *Trusting What You Have Trained*   49

CHAPTER 4: *Self-confidence From The Inside-Out*   75

CHAPTER 5: *Managing Your Attentional Focus*   103

CHAPTER 6: *Creating a Positive Performance Mindset*   121

CHAPTER 7: *Designing Your Performance Future*   149

CHAPTER 8: *Making It Happen*   163

Preface

A few years back I received a phone call from the Dean of the School of Music asking me to give a presentation to his graduate faculty and students at the University of Oklahoma. He wanted me to talk about the techniques and strategies used in sport psychology and how they could be used to enhance the performance of musicians. Little did I know at the time how much this phone call would change my life.

Although, I had spent the previous 20 years as a sport psychology consultant working with coaches, athletes, and business professionals, I had limited experience working with musicians and very little familiarity with the music culture. My first presentation to the School of Music was entitled, "Blue Twisted Steel: Mental Toughness Training for Musicians." I felt this facetious title was needed to convey a sense of humor regarding my lack of musical training (Years prior, a football coach pointed out that blue twisted steel was the hardest steel available and that is what he wanted his players to become). After that presentation, I began teaching a graduate class in performance psychology for musicians. For many years now, I have been teaching this class while giving presentations to various music conferences and conducting workshops for music teachers and performers. These experiences provided me with a performance laboratory, of sorts, to learn and experiment with what works in helping musicians perform their best when it counts. This book is a result of the years I have spent applying strategies for enhancing the performance of musicians at a variety of developmental levels.

Introduction:
Parallel Paths To Excellence

"We call music a performing art, although musicians spend comparatively little time on the stage. The vast majority of a musician's life is spent preparing to perform. We are, in fact, not performers but "practicers" who go before the public from time to time."

- John Minahan, *The Art and Science of Practicing*

Without a doubt, the most surprising difference between athletes and musicians is not the amount of time spent practicing, but the amount of time spent playing. Most competitive athletes have dozens of performance repetitions over the course of six months, while most musicians may have one or two. For the most part, athletes are "players" who practice while musicians are "practicers" who play. This has implications for the way musicians best transfer what is learned in practice to their performances.

To play your best when it counts, you must simultaniously walk two parallel paths. One path for the development and refinement of your technical and musical skills, and a second path for the development and refinement of your mental performance skills. This book is designed to help you walk this second path. It will help you better understand your mental performance skills, teach you how to practice them, and help you execute them during performance.

When aerospace engineers started experimenting with supersonic flight, they quickly realized they had to radically change the way they thought. The wing shape and nose cones of subsonic planes had to be changed to accommodate the laws of physics at supersonic flight; laws much different from subsonic flight. If they wanted to move into this brave new level of flight, these scientists had to embrace and adjust to the realities operating at this level. Similarly, if musicians want to move from being great practicers to great performers, a new level of thinking is required. Different rules apply to *learning* music than apply to *performing* music. In other words, "putting it in" and "getting it out" are two entirely different processes with two entirely different sets of rules. To accomplish a more effective transfer of training from practice to performance, you must not only change how you practice but what you practice.

From a psychological perspective, practicing to perform is not the same as practicing to improve. The mental skills needed to be a great practicer are not the same mental skills needed to be a great performer. In fact, the mental skills necessary to develop and refine your technique will get in your way during performance. I am not implying becoming more technically or musically proficient will not make you a better performer. Rather, there are two separate and distinct "sets" of mental skills needed to reach your full performance potential. One set of skills for acquisition and another set for performance. Practicing your mental performance skills is necessary for playing your best. Once you make a commitment to practicing your performance skills, you will become a more confident performer and have more consistent performances, while rediscovering the joy and meaning found in playing your best.

Most teachers and coaches know a lot about how technical skills are learned. They know about creating an optimal learning environment, designing practice formats to maximize learning, using various types of feedback to accommodate different learning styles, and implementing teaching aids and drills to facilitate skill acquisition. They also understand if you truly want to get better, then you must develop your ability to self-monitor correctness, understand and analyze cause-and-effect relationships relative to technical mistakes, and self-instruct during practice sessions. These are the mental skills necessary for developing and refining your technical and musical skills. There will never be a magical point at which time you no longer have to self-instruct or monitor correctness. There will always be something you must learn or refine to keep improving, but there are other mental skills needed to get out during performance what you have already put in during practice.

PLAYING YOUR BEST WHEN IT COUNTS

Think of the best performers you have known in sport, performing arts, or business. What are the psychological skills they share? How did they develop these skills and how can others acquire them? These are common questions posed by the field of performance psychology. In a nut shell, performance psychology is a positive approach to studying human performance, both in group and individual performance settings. Through a better understanding of great performers and their performances, we can develop coaching and training methods for enhancing performance in others.

Almost every high-level performer has, at some time, either experienced or heard about the "flow state," or playing "in the zone." Many performers such as yourself have experienced moments when you entered into a mindset where you felt totally focused, calm, confident, and completely able to execute even the most difficult skills with ease. Those moments in which time seemed to stand still and conscious effort was nonexistent. If you have had this type of experience you would likely do just about anything to get back there but probably do not know how. If you have not had the experience of being in the zone, you may have wondered how to get into that mindset or worried about why you have never been there. This book will help you develop the performance mindset necessary for playing your best under pressure.

THE PERFORMANCE MINDSET

As your technique moves through the stages of skill development it becomes more refined, resulting in more efficient and automatic movement sequences. Scientists recognize this "motor program refinement" as a shift from movements requiring conscious effort and monitoring, to the smoother execution of complex movements that unfold with little conscious control. In other words, as your technique becomes well-learned and complex, your conscious mind must become less involved or, as suggested in the quote below, you must release conscious control over correctness and trust the motor programs you have trained in practice:

"Ultimately, the musician must relinquish the illusion of moment-by-moment control, trusting the program to remember exactly how each finger must move. The musician becomes aware of only the feeling, the emotion in the music."

. . . Dr. Frank Wilson, neurologist

Your best performances occur when you are totally absorbed in and connected to the task at hand: free from expectations, fears, doubts and other cognitive activity. In essence, you trust yourself and what you have trained. When you trust, you are letting go of conscious control and allowing natural, well-trained processes to execute the skill. A trusting mindset is necessary to access your best performance state allowing you to sustain high levels of performance. This letting go process is not free from cognitive interference and can be interrupted by factors causing the conscious mind to disrupt the performance process. Self-doubt, fear of mistakes, over-analysis of technique and heightened anxiety are examples of cognitions that interrupt the automatic transfer of information necessary to execute your motor programs. Trust during performance is a mindset you can achieve on purpose and with greater frequency than you do now.

USING THIS BOOK

You will find the material in this book to be applicable to your performance reality. Each chapter leads you to think about and apply the information directly to your practices and performances. Throughout this book you will be asked to reflect upon specific topic areas and write down your thoughts regarding your current and/or past performances. Take time to reflect upon your understandings and experiences while you read and challenge yourself to be open and honest with your responses.

The paper margins of this book allow room for you to write your thoughts and notes as you go through the chapters. At the end of each chapter, you will find *Self-Reflection Questions* for you to complete before moving onto the next chapter. Some of these questions are designed to provide you with an understanding of how to apply the material covered, while others prepare you for the material in the following chapter.

Keep in mind, this book challenges you to explore important performance issues and develop specific psychological skills. However, a continued commitment to the development of the technical and musical aspects of your performance will only make this training more effective.

Playing Your Best Journal

You will find it helpful to keep the *Playing Your Best High-performance Journal* as you apply the material in this book (www.playingyourbest.com). The High-performance Journal is an important tool for you to use to keep you on track with your goals and to monitor improvements in your mental performance skills. This mental journal may be the most important and meaningful activity you engage in as you work through the chapters in this book. If you have never kept this type of journal before, I ask that you approach it with an open mind and give it your best shot.

Playing Your Best Workbook

The *Playing Your Best Workbook* was created as a supplement to this book. It consists of extensive self-awareness and application activities developed and refined over many years of teaching Performance Psychology classes to music students. The workbook provides a solid foundation for developing the mental performance skills found in this book.

POSTSCRIPT

In today's high pressure performance environments, a thoughtful and integrated approach to the development of a positive and trusting mindset is necessary. When you are stronger mentally and emotionally, you are able to perform with more energy, passion and purpose for longer periods of time. How do you practice these mental performance skills in practice? This book was created with this question in mind. This book is designed to provide a solid foundation for playing your best when it counts by helping you to:

- Change self-limiting beliefs and attitudes.
- Trust during performance what you trained in practice.
- Develop a positive performance mindset.
- Practice and improve mental performance skills.
- Instill greater confidence in yourself as a musician.
- Create and achieve a performance future of your choosing.

SELF-REFLECTION QUESTIONS

To begin your journey in developing and refining your mental performance skills reflect upon the following questions and write your responses in the space provided.

1. Why do you perform? What is it about performing your music that really turns you on?

   _____

   _____

   _____

   _____

   _____

   _____

   _____

2. What are your key performance goals for this year (e.g., perform a solo recital, enter a concerto competition)?

   1. _____
   2. _____
   3. _____
   4. _____

3. What mental skills would you like to improve (e.g., trust my technique, sharpen my focus, overcome fear of memory slips)?

   1. _____
   2. _____
   3. _____
   4. _____

4. Reflect upon an image of you performing at your best (e.g., puppy dog). Then use vivid language to describe the specific characteristics of this image representing you at your best (e.g., free, spontaneous, creative, having fun), and explain what each of these characteristics mean to you as a performer.

   "When I am at my best during performance, I am like a. . . .

   "_____."

   Why does this represents my best? What are the characteristics that represent me at my best? Explain why.

   1. _____
   2. _____
   3. _____
   4. _____

5. What are the barriers that keep you from playing your best more consistently (e.g., self-doubt, negative thinking, fear of being judged)?

   1. _____

   2. _____

   3. _____

   4. _____

   5. _____

1
Harnessing Your Passion To Perform

The Hound and The Hare

A hare was nibbling away at some plants in a field one day when she noticed a hunter she had never seen before patrolling the area with his hound.

Now I have two new predators to outwit, the animal thought, and since that hound is a lot younger than I am, he's probably a lot faster too. To offset the hound's speed, I'll need to know every inch of terrain by heart.

Seizing the initiative, the hare went out to the fields at suppertime when she knew the hunter was not around. She studied every hiding place, every briar, and the path through every bramble. A few days later, the hound spotted the hare and gave chase. The hare darted through the fields, briars, and underbrush and she easily escaped. Tired and disappointed, the hound returned to the hunter.

A goat passing by saw the whole chase and began to berate the hound. "Some hunter you turned out to be! You ought to be ashamed of yourself, letting a hare so much smaller and older get the better of you."

"You're forgetting one thing," the hound replied. "I was running for my supper, but that hare was running for her life."

I remember the first time I saw an athlete cry after winning a major championship. It was Bjorn Borg falling to his knees after winning his fifth Wimbledon title. As a young tennis player myself I could not help but wonder what it must feel like to break down and cry after *winning* a match. I had cried after losing but never after winning. Yet, Bjorn Borg, aka "The Iceman," the one player who had never shown emotion before, during or after matches, fell to his knees, covered his face and cried in front of millions of people. I wanted to feel what he felt. I wanted to feel that pure, honest emotion of joy that exists at the intersection of hard work, passion, and finally, success.

After years of competing in junior, intercollegiate and professional tennis, I never cried after winning a match. I found myself to be much more like the hare in the story. I worked hard, studied my opponents and had great coaching, but it seemed like I was always running for my life. Winning was more of a relief than a joy. It was the fear of failing that harnessed my energy and focus to perform. Today, I still compete in tennis and golf, play and practice piano, but I am driven more out of my love for the challenge inherent in performance than by the fear of failing.

How often do you rely on the fear of negative consequences to concentrate your power and get the job done? In the case of the hare, her commitment to staying alive resulted in her "seizing the initiative" and concentrating her efforts to "outwit" her predators. There is no doubt fear works to mobilize our efforts. What if you were able to draw from a more positive energy source when achieving your goals? An energy source that *pulls* you toward a goal rather than *pushes* you.

I have found it helpful to understand passion as an energy source helping to direct actions and providing positive feelings associated with completing tasks. Think of passion and fear as opposite ends of the same continuum. On one hand, fear mobilizes when trying to avoid negative consequences (Although fear is a negative motivator, it is a motivator nonetheless). On the other hand, passion is a positive motivator equally effective in mobilizing your effort. When a goal is the object of your passion you are energized and inspired to achieve it. You are pulled toward it. This is not to suggest you must become passionate about everything you do.

There are times when fear is necessary to do something you really do not want to do. Using the positive energy found in passion is a skill you can learn. Harnessing your passion to perform is a good first step to playing your best when it counts.

This chapter will teach you to use the power of passion to generate positive enthusiasm for accomplishing your performance goals. To have a personal quest for attaining something you truly *desire*. Unlike the hare, it is a commitment to a goal out of love, not fear!

PASSIONATE COMMITMENT

"Far better to dare mighty things, to win glorious triumphs, even though checkered by failure, than to rank with those poor spirits who neither enjoy much nor suffer much, because they live in the grey twilight that knows neither victory nor defeat."

. . . Theodore Roosevelt

This quote captures the risks and rewards of believing in yourself and pushing the limits of your talents. The greatest accomplishments in your life will usually begin with a personal dare to dream of something great. It takes courage and commitment to truly go after your dreams and 'win glorious triumphs.' One thing is for certain, when you honestly invest in, care about, and commit to lofty goals, you will enjoy much but you will also suffer much. Choosing to fully invest in your dream and go after something big in your life is a choice to believe in yourself, engage in a positive process, and face your fears. Ultimately, you must decide for yourself if it is 'Far better to dare mighty things,' or not. If you are willing to do whatever you can to become a better, more engaged and more passionate musician, then this book is for you.

Even though great accomplishments throughout history have grown out of fear, many times the ultimate goal was achieved out of passion. For example, the quest for a nuclear bomb was motivated out of fear. But the scientist and engineers on the ground were passionate about solving the problem. The same may be said about the space program landing a man on the moon and returning him safely to earth. In both cases, there was a commitment to something big and a passionate drive to achieve it. Sure, the consequences of failure were great and there were many failures along the way but, the passionate commitment to achieve something never done before was the driving force for the men and women doing the work.

Passionate commitment is the key to quality in any human endeavor. Whether it is a quality painting, a beautifully written piece of music, or an effortless golf swing. Even the untrained eye can appreciate the time, energy, and focus required to produce a quality product. This type of commitment is a personal pledge not to just "get the job done," but to do it with pride, passion, and perseverance. It is committed, caring musicians who generate and deliver signature performances on a consistent basis.

When was the last time you produced something of quality without caring about doing it well? You cannot have quality without caring. Of course, there are different ways to commit your efforts. Some people commit out of obligation. Others commit because it is in their value set to follow-through on a task or to do what they said they were going to do. Nothing is especially *wrong* with either of these approaches, but they do not have the potential to truly excite your passion, energize your will, or engage your heart. Commitment to do great things does not come without the risk of failure. To truly commit to achieve a goal, to concentrate your power and focus, you must embrace the risks and choose courage over fear.

Let us be honest. If you are going to jump wholeheartedly into being a great performer, then you are going to need all the positive emotion you can generate, all the will you can muster, and all the "heart" you can find! Real, wholehearted commitment means you will have to make sacrifices. You will most likely have to make adjustments in your lifestyle. You will absolutely have to give up some things currently making your life comfortable or easy. Real commitment abandons comfort and ease! Real commitment goes further, digs deeper and stays longer than you ever have before!

PASSION AS THE MOTHER OF DISCIPLINE

How can passion direct your energy and intensify your efforts? Think of a child playing with trucks in a sandbox. Notice how the child becomes the little people inside the trucks, moving the dirt, talking to each other, and coordinating their actions to get the job done. The child's fascination enables a natural connection between him and the task at hand. An outside observer might even marvel at the child's "disciplined focus" and "precise movements" but in reality the child is not trying to be "correct," he or she is simply being "the truck driver" or being "the truck." Although, passion looks a lot like discipline from the outside, it feels very different on the inside.

I remember growing up in Florida practicing my tennis serve in the middle of the afternoon and hitting tennis balls against the practice wall for hours at a time. I would pretend I was Stan Smith serving an ace on match point or Rod Laver running down a wide backhand and hitting a winner cross court. Then one day while sitting in our family room, I overheard an adult friend of my parents comment on how disciplined I was to practice so much in the hot sun. The comment struck me by surprise and my reaction is one I remember to this day. I started laughing! I was laughing at what I thought was one of the dumbest things I had ever heard. I was laughing because deep down, I understood two things to be true: one, I was the least disciplined person in the world and two, my practicing tennis in the hot sun had nothing to do with being disciplined. You see, I loved hitting tennis balls. I loved practicing in the afternoons because no one else was around to bother me. I could win all the imaginary championships I wanted, free of interruptions! I loved getting better at tennis – hitting the ball more solid and hitting more precise targets. I loved the challenge of playing well against different opponents and feeling exhausted after a match. There was nothing I would rather be doing than that! Discipline was mowing the lawn on Saturday morning, washing dishes after dinner, cleaning out the car, or doing homework. Discipline is doing what you do not want to do when you do not want to do it. I was anything but disciplined. Once I figured out my parents believed practicing tennis was a sign of self-discipline, I was able to get out of almost all of my chores because, "I had to go practice and I didn't have time to mow the lawn."

Then it happened. I am not sure if it was a gradual process that took place over time or if I just woke up one day and realized other people cared how well I played. Coaches, teachers, neighbors, friends and family members all seemed to be invested in my performances. I was now expected to play well, expected to win, and bring home the trophy. This reality changed the *reason* I played tennis. I became more critical of my performances, more judgmental of my mistakes and more frustrated with my weaknesses. The good news is I became more self-disciplined but, in the process, I also lost the joy and passion for performing.

GOING AFTER YOUR BEST

Why do you do what you do? This question gets at the heart of motivation. There are many things you do to avoid the consequences of not doing them. For example, doing homework is rarely something you are drawn to do out of interest. For many people, working at their jobs is something they would choose not to do if they did not need to make a living. Extrinsic motivation is doing something because you are either avoiding an external punishment (bad grade) or seeking an external reward (money). In other words, your motives for completing a task are extrinsic or external to you. This is different from being internally motivated.

When you read a chapter in a book because you are interested in learning the material or when you work at a task because you genuinely want to feel the satisfaction of doing a good job, you are motivated by intrinsic factors. When someone is passionate about what they are doing they are motivated by the intrinsic value of the activity. When I was playing tennis in my youth, I was passionate about mastering the technical, strategic, and mental aspects of the game. Winning a match, tournament or trophy was an important indication of my progress. Competing against other players was enjoyable but my true passion was in the process of mastery.

Many young performers start out with a similar passion. As they get better and move to higher levels of performance or competition their motivation as well as the motivation of the people around them, starts to shift to more extrinsic rewards. They start emphasizing a higher ranking, greater exposure, college scholarship, or even financial rewards. Often, this emphasis on extrinsic rewards starts to replace the intrinsic value of the activity and then it begins to "feel like a job." Over time, the value of extrinsic rewards becomes the primary motivator and the love of the game gets lost in the process.

The use of extrinsic rewards may help to motivate behavior in the initial stages but once rewards become the primary motivator, passion for doing the activity is diminished. This motivational shift from intrinsic to extrinsic is evident in the story of the old man whose afternoon nap kept getting interrupted by a group of boys who enjoyed playing outside his bedroom window. One day, the old man gathered the boys and said he would pay them a dollar a day for playing in his yard after school. After doing so for a week, he brought them back together and said he was running a little short on money and wondered if they would play in his yard for only fifty cents. After a short conference the boys decided they would. The following week, the old man gathered the boys again and said he could only pay them one quarter each. At that point, the boys decided one quarter a day was not enough money and they refused to play in his yard ever again. As you can see, once the boys started playing in the old man's yard for money the intrinsic reward (fun) was replaced by the extrinsic reward (money), and once that reward was taken away, there was no reason to do it anymore, much to the satisfaction of the old man who preferred uninterrupted naps!

In our culture, the use of rewards as motivators is evident in all occupations. Consumer products, companies, school systems, and corporations all use rewards as primary motivators. This is not to suggest that rewards are bad or that they do not motivate behavior, only that they can change the reason for doing what you are doing. Alternatively, passion is developed by emphasizing the intrinsic value of an activity. So, if you want to become more passionately committed to your goals, you must first connect to the intrinsic value of the activities needed to accomplish that goal.

CONNECTING WITH YOUR PASSION

As a musician, when you are connected with, and playing out of passion, you are not focused on your mistakes or weaknesses, but on solutions. In other words, you enjoy what you are doing well and do not get stuck or fixated on what you are not doing well. Harnessing your passion to perform begins with reconnecting to the joy and the love of playing your music, the feeling of expressing yourself and connecting with your audience. Many musicians lose their passion to perform as a result of being in a culture fixated on eliminating mistakes and improving weaknesses. Over time, musicians grow to become highly self-critical, judgmental and analytical, causing self-limiting beliefs and negativity dominate their thinking. As a result, they lose their connection with the passion and joy they once had when both practicing and performing their music.

If you are like most musicians you probably spend more time thinking about the bad things that happened in practice or what went wrong with your performance than the good things. You have learned to vividly recall the negative aspects rather than the positive aspects of practices and performances. If you want to harness your passion to perform then you must *retrain* your ability to think about and recall the great things you do. Two proven strategies for doing just that are using performance scripts and mental journals.

A performance script is a wonderful way to create vivid memories, images and sensations of what it feels like to play great. Having these sensations and images of playing great readily available to your memory, free you from the shackles of negativism and allow you to play with the joy and passion found in your best performances.

Keeping a mental journal is powerful source you can draw from to reconnect with your passion. Unlike other journals, your mental journal is designed to help you organize your time and prioritize your training activities while keeping you accountable to doing what you need to be doing to perform your very best. This strength-focused approach is fundamental to harnessing your passion. When you focus on the things you do well, the best aspects of a practice session or a particular performance, you will tap into the joy and passion in your music. You will work more intensely and for longer periods of time with more enjoyment.

MAKING A PERFORMANCE SCRIPT

A performance script is a description of the sensations you experience when you are playing great! Performance scripts are used to create a feeling of certainty and confidence about your performance. The goal of a performance script is to create a vivid representation of a near perfect performance. When done well, your script includes a vivid and rich description of the sensations (sights, sounds, and smells) and emotions (excitement, confidence, and enjoyment) you experience when playing your best in a particular venue.

PERFORMANCE SCRIPT FORMAT

Below is a suggested format for writing your performance script along with an example of each of the five sections: performance location, warm-up, beginning your performance, middle of your performance, and finishing your performance.

Performance Location

To begin your script, describe where you are, the time of day and any special sounds or smells. Your performance location might be your favorite place to play, the venue of your last great performance, or the site of an upcoming one. Recall or create, in detail, the images present. Paint a picture with your words, be as vivid as you can!

"The sun is shining, which makes the cold a little more bearable. I'm dressed in layers so I'm keeping warm. My breath also keeps me warm and relaxed. I enter the church and it smells of aged wood and old carpet. The carpet is bright red. I walk into the performance space and it is totally empty. The light is bright and the wood glistens in the light. I see the piano, it is a black Yamaha. I also see gold candelabras; the candles are not lit. All the large wooden doors are closed. I am amazed by the silence and I embrace it!"

Warm-up Routine

Describe how you are feeling and thinking during your onsite warm-up. How great it feels to be where you are and feeling ready to perform. Everything is going great in warm-up and you are feeling just the way you want before your performance.

"My hands are warm, and they are moving freely. I begin playing several scales and arpeggios. The blood is flowing freely in my arms and hands and I feel no tension. I am able to take deep breaths and to play the exercises musically. I feel myself breathing. I feel warm and ready to play. I start playing the beginnings of each of my pieces. I play them slowly at first, very relaxed and deliberate. I then establish a performance tempo for each of them. I go and get a drink and prepare myself for the performance."

Beginning Your Performance

Describe what it feels like to get off to a great start. What are the mental and physical elements needed for a great beginning to your performance? Draw upon past great starts and describe the feelings. How great it is to feel so confident and energized. Describe how well you execute your technique with composure and how your confidence is starting to build.

"I walk out and hear the people applaud. As I walk, I smile warmly, but inside I am breathing and preparing myself to begin my first piece. As I sit down, I focus on my breath, I sing the opening melody in my head, and I begin to play. I feel relaxed, and I am enjoying the tone of the piano in this large space. The hall is silent to me. I do not hear people moving or children talking. I finish the Scarlatti Sonatas, and I feel confident and relaxed. I move into the Beethoven Sonata. I hear the opening chord in my head before I play it. The sound is warm, and yet it projects to the back of the hall. As I move into the Allegro section, I feel the inner pulse, and I move easily into the 3rd's passage. I take a relaxed breath, and I release the breath as I ascend into this passage. I feel relaxed and secure. In the second movement, I can hear the melody floating across the slower tempo. I can feel Beethoven's tempo and his sense of loss in this movement. As I transition into the 3rd movement, my body feels relaxed and yet has the strength to project the opening passage with clarity. I feel the joy and ease in this opening melody. I express that in my playing of it. I never lose the sense of pulse, it is constantly beating in my core."

Middle Of Your Performance

Imagine a perfect performance. Everything is working. You are focused and relaxed. Nothing is bothering you. You are flowing and letting it go. It is a great feeling to be so positive about all aspects of your performance. You are connecting with your audience. It all seems so effortless and natural.

"I leave for intermission. I leave confident and full of joy. I sit in my dressing room and think of nothing for a few minutes. I feel totally relaxed and ready to begin and start to think about the second half. I walk out confidently to start my set of Nocturnes. I have nothing on my mind but the desire to make beautiful music. My mind is focused and clear. For each Nocturne, I hear the sound that I want to produce before I play each opening passage. I am expressive and enjoying the music that is coming out of me."

Finishing Your Performance

Visualize a strong finish. You have all the momentum and you are supremely confident. You are completely focused on the task at hand. Nothing is distracting you. You complete your performance with positive emotion, and you feel great!

"I feel strong and ready to play this exciting piece. I feel the dance rhythms before I begin. As I start to play, I am aware of my l.h. As I finish the 1st movement, my arms feel strong but not tight, they feel relaxed enough to start playing the 2nd movement. I start the 2nd movement I am amazed at the sound that is flowing out; it sounds like a musical whisper. The room is silent as I begin my 3rd movement I have a controlled sense of rage, an emotion that I feel the composer desires to communicate with this movement. I am effortlessly matching the composer's feelings. The climax builds gradually. I breathe, while letting go of some of the excitement, letting the intensity flow. I end with a soft, ringing sound. The last movement begins. The rhythm is clear and precise. I move effortlessly between the different sections and leaps. I inhale and exhale with a shallow breath while maintaining intensity and control. As I flow into the exciting conclusion, I imagine warm fluid flowing through my arms keeping me relaxed and my muscles loose. I nail the concluding octave and the

audience is excited with their applause. I walk off feeling confident and grateful for another opportunity to perform. I am smiling."

Although, reading someone else's performance script does not create the same feelings inside you that reading your own does, you can begin to understand the freedom, passion and joy it creates. To experience the full effect of a performance script, you must write your own. To begin your own script, I recommend you simply sit down and start writing. Recall the feelings of playing great from past performances and use your imagination to include very rich sensory language and feelings. For best results, develop one performance script using the above format. From that script you can make adjustments to meet the specific demands of subsequent performances using the performance script sheets in your High-performance Journal.

It is helpful to keep in mind that visualization is a skill and, like other skills, you can improve it over time. With just a few minutes of practice, a couple of times each week, you can get better at creating and controlling vivid images. At first, it might seem effortful and somewhat frustrating because your images may be very fuzzy and hard to control but, as you practice, you will notice your images becoming more vivid and controllable and the process more effortless and enjoyable. With just 5 to 10 minutes of visualization practice three days a week, you will notice significant improvement. Think of it like beginning a fitness program. The first week or two is hard, but you progress rapidly and once you get a baseline fitness level, your workouts become more enjoyable.

KEEPING A MENTAL JOURNAL

For years, successful performers from a variety of domains (business, sport, performing arts) have used mental journals with positive effects on their personal development and their performance outcomes. Keeping a mental journal not only allows you to monitor improvement of your psychological skills, it also enables you to record solutions and reflect upon the positive aspects of both your practices and performances. Thousands of successful musicians have used mental journals to guide them down the path of personal excellence. For hundreds of years sailors have used journals to help them navigate treacherous waters and keep them on track to reaching their destinations. Similarly, your journal is a tool for you to monitor your improvement and record the very best of what you are doing with the purpose of keeping you positively focused on, and passionately committed to, your performance goals.

The High-performance Journal is a tool for you to use as a means of training yourself to be strength-focused and solution-oriented. If you truly desire to push the limits of your talents, then keeping this mental journal will be both meaningful and rewarding. Keeping this journal is a way of saying to yourself that you care about performing your best and you are serious about accomplishing your goals. Use the High-performance Journal for four weeks and see what happens! This journal will enhance your belief in your capabilities as a performer and help you to fully commit yourself to getting to the next level. It is specifically designed to provide you with a foundation from which to harness your passion and build confidence in yourself.

The *Playing Your Best: High-performance Journal* is a spiral bound notebook consisting of both practice and performance journals. It is designed this way to be easily accessible to you so that you can make new entries and refer to previous entries when necessary. You will find that your journal entries will often build on one another and that there will be frequently recurring questions or evolving ideas that appear across several of your entries. When you make journal entries, write in a way you find comfortable for accomplishing your goals for each section. The length of each entry depends on you and on what you want to write about regarding your specific practice session and/or performance. The following is a description of each of the practice and performance journal sections of your High-performance Journal.

PRACTICE JOURNAL INSTRUCTIONS

Your practice journal will keep you focused on things you need to be doing to improve and positive about the things you are doing well. Your practice journal is a record of your practice goals, activities and thoughts about what went well during each practice session. You may want to include comments about how you worked through difficult situations, specific problems you met, and solutions to those problem. Many of the things you write in your journal are completely up to you. However, I recommend you commit to using the format suggested below for at least two weeks. After that time, you may wish to adjust your writing and format to a style that best suits you.

Weekly Plan

At the beginning of each week plan your practices for each day. Specifically, your goals for each practice, the activities needed to accomplish those goals, and the estimated time for each activity. At first this may seem to be a daunting task. However, over time, you will become more proficient at identifying meaningful goals and activities. Your weekly plan is not written in stone! It is expected that each week you will make certain adjustments based on what was accomplished in the previous days. It is very important that you become skilled at estimating the amount of time you spend doing each of the specific activities. By doing so you will be much more efficient with your time. This will help you better organize each practice session and get the most out of them.

Daily Practice Journal

This is your opportunity to write down your goals before practice and record the best aspects following practice. Do not get discouraged if you miss a few days just pick up where you left off. You may also decide to make journal entries every other day. Your mental practice journal will help you organize your time and prioritize your training activities. It will keep you accountable doing what you need to be doing to perform your best.

Practice Situation: This is where you indicate the location of your practice and your overall mood at the beginning of practice and after practice. This will provide you with a measure of your mood states. Although many musicians report they dread practice, they also report some of their most meaningful experiences occur when they are engaged in their practice.

My Goals Today: Write down the specific goals you want to accomplish before each practice session. This will help you think through what is important and stay focused during practice.

Best Aspects of Today's Practice: Following your practice session, take some time to reflect upon the specific things you liked and did well. These could be mental, physical, technical or musical. The goal of this section is to develop the habit of thinking about and vividly recalling your successes or the things you are doing well.

Best Solutions: In this section, record the challenges or problems that arose during each practice session and the solution(s) you implemented to overcome them. You might describe a specific technical solution, particular musical decision you made, or solution to a mental challenge that occurred during your performance. The goal of this section is to train yourself to think of solutions instead of just focusing on problems.

Things to Remember: Write down a few specific things from your practice session you feel you would benefit from remembering. These could be solutions to specific challenges or just reminders you want to look over before next practice. This will help you keep on track and remember what you need to be working on during your next practice.

Daily Personal Journal

Your daily journal is a place for you to reflect upon the memorable things that took place that day. There is no tried-and-true format for this type of writing. Write for just a few minutes at the end of the day about whatever stands out or is on your mind.

Food Log: This provides a very brief place to monitor the nutritional aspect of being a high performer. It allows you to rate how well you did that day in following your nutritional goals.

What I am Most Thankful For Today: This is where you want to include comments about what you are thankful for that day. Many of the things you write in this section are completely up to you. If you commit to writing in this section you will begin to experience the benefits of a more positive mindset.

Goals for Tomorrow: The last section challenges you to reflect upon and identify one to five specific goals you will accomplish tomorrow. Writing down these goals at the end of a practice session while they are fresh in your mind will help guide you for the next practice.

Weekly Key Points and Solutions

At the end of each week you will find it helpful to summarize or record the key points you want to remember from that week and any solutions you found meaningful. This will be important as you are developing your performance piece(s) by proving you a place you can easily refer to for important reminders needed for the following week.

Weekly Notes and Reminders

This section is designed to assist you in recording any thoughts you have during a practice session you may want to refer to later or develop in greater detail. By writing your thoughts down in the moment you are able to keep working on a specific practice activity without fear of forgetting the thought you may need to return to later.

PERFORMANCE JOURNAL INSTRUCTIONS

A performance journal provides you the opportunity to prepare for, and reflect on, performances in ways that enhance your confidence. It trains you to approach and respond to performance situations in positive ways. A performance journal provides a structured format for building on the best aspects of your performances. This structure consists of four sections: 1. Performance plan: consisting of your performance goals and game plan, 2. Performance script: a vivid description of the sensations of playing great, 3. Performance notes: reminders and key points that may be developed the day before or during rehearsal, and 4. Post-performance evaluation: providing the opportunity to recall and reflect upon the best aspects of your performance. Below is a brief description of the performance journal entries.

Performance Plan

Begin your performance journal entry by describing the performance situation. This would include a description of the event, location, purpose and other notable features of the performance situation. Then identify one to four goals for your performance. It is best to keep these goals focused on those things over which you have control. For example, self-coaching, decisiveness, acceptance of mistakes, and courage to trust what you have. All great performers have a plan going into their performance. This part of your performance journal challenges you to develop specific performance goals and think through a game plan for your performance. Understand what you did to effectively prepare yourself for this performance and draw from this understanding for your next performance.

Performance Script

You will have the opportunity to develop a performance script for each of your performances. Remember, your performance script is a description of the sensations of playing great! The goal of a this script is to create a vivid representation of a near perfect performance. Read it regularly during the days leading up to your performance.

Performance Notes

Your performance notes should consist of any key points or adjustments you need to remember. For example, you might have a few aspects of your performance piece you worked out during practice and want to be sure to include in your performance. There may also be some information from rehearsal that you need to keep in mind during your performance. This section is a place to keep those notes but be sure to make them brief and easy to remember.

Post-Performance Evaluation

Your post-performance evaluation provides you the opportunity to think through those things you did well and to develop vivid memories you can use in subsequent performances. Even if you do not get the opportunity to complete all the sections of your journal before your performance, take the time to complete your post-performance evaluation. However, you will find all aspects of your performance journal to be a valuable asset in your development of a positive performance mindset.

Performance Situation: Write down the date of your performance, location, conditions, and perceived difficulty of the piece(s) you are playing.

Pre-Performance Warm-up: Write down some of your meaningful warm-up activities that helped you prepare for this performance. You should also record any notable events that took place before your performance for you to either avoid or include in your preparation routine. The goal of this section is to have an understanding of what you did to effectively prepare yourself for this performance and to draw from this for your next performance.

Best Aspects of My Performance: Here is where you recall and record as vividly as you can the best aspects of your performance, and what you liked or did exceptionally well. Some examples include; the best aspects of the beginning, the middle, and the end of your performance, best passage, best musical expression, best technical execution and best recovery. The goal is to make these aspects more vivid and accessible to your memory so you can recall them during subsequent performances.

Best Solutions: This section is where you record the challenges or problems that arose during this performance and the solution(s) you implemented to overcome them. You might describe a specific technical solution, or a particular musical decision you made, or a solution to a mental challenge that occurred during your performance. The goal of this section is to train yourself to think of solutions during performance instead of problems.

What I Enjoyed Most About this Performance: Think back to your performance and ask, "What did I enjoy most about this performance?" You may have worked through a period of frustration, persisted through a series of distractions, successfully refocused after an early performance mistake, or stayed positive and relaxed down the stretch. Remember, the goal is to make these aspects more vivid and accessible to your memory so you can recall them during subsequent performances.

Things to Remember: Your performance evaluation should end with reminders to take with you or to look back upon. These can be short statements that address specific things about the physical, mental, technical or musical aspects of your performance that you want to be sure to remember for your next practice session or next performance.

POSTSCRIPT

In many aspects of music performance there are sequential stages in the developmental process resulting in learning and implementation of new skills or new material. For example, when you engage in a specific sequence of activities used to memorize a new piece of music. Similarly, the development of mental skills requires a series of stages before they can be fully implemented into your performances.

Just as there are no short cuts to lasting success in music, there are no short cuts in the development of mental skills. Many aspects of physical practice assist in the development of mental skills and simulating performance pressure in practice helps transition to the performance environment. But physical practice and simulation alone are not sufficient for most musicians to reach the high levels of confidence, concentration, and composure needed to consistently play their best when it counts. Although many musicians develop the necessary mental skills to be successful, a systematic, structured method for mental skills development insures that these skills will not be left up to a "trial and error." If you are required to consistently perform at your peak level in high stress environments then you must develop the mental skills allowing you to play your best not just for one performance, but for the length of your career.

SELF-REFLECTION QUESTIONS

1. Describe four situations in which you have had trouble creating a positive attitude (e.g., unmotivated for practice, not happy about rehearsal). Develop a strategy to use to get back into your positive mindset (e.g., set focus goals, speak up during rehearsal)

Situations	Strategies

2. Start making practice and performance entries in your high-performance journal. Follow the format for at least ten days and two performances. Once you have had experience with this type of journal writing you may adjust it to better suit your personal style.

3. Develop a Performance Script. Type your performance script following the format and guidelines presented in this chapter. Record your feelings, thoughts and emotions by drawing on past best performances to create the feeling of playing great.

4. Think about the last year of your life. During this year, have you been passionate about your development as a musician? If your answer is yes, describe what it means for you to have passion. If your answer is no, describe what is lacking and what you need to harness your passion to perform. You may find it helpful to compare the attitude you had as a child dreaming about a particular future to your current attitude. Think about the experiences and people in your life that have caused your passion

to diminish (e.g., self-doubt, fear, becoming overly serious, analytical and self-conscious). How has your thinking held you back from being the best you can be? How have your concerns about being respected, and winning the approval of others, affected your passion toward practicing and performing?

My Passionate Attitude

2
Mental Skills For Musicians

The Blind Men and the Elephant

Beyond Ghor there was a city. All its inhabitants were blind. A king with his entourage arrived nearby; he brought his army and camped in the desert. He had a mighty elephant which he used in attack to increase the people's awe.

The populace became eager to learn about the elephant and some scientists from this blind community went to find it. Since they did not know even the form or shape of the elephant, they groped sightlessly, gathering information by touching some part of it. Each thought he knew something, because he could feel a part.

When they returned to their fellow citizens, eager groups clustered around them, anxious, to learn the truth from those who were themselves astray. They asked about the form and shape of the elephant and listened to all they were told.

The scientist whose hand had reached an ear said, "It is a large, rough thing, wide and broad, like a rug." One who had felt the trunk said, "I have the real facts about it. It is like a straight and hollow pipe, awful and destructive." One who had felt its feet and legs said, "It is mighty and firm, like a pillar."

Each had felt one part out of many. Each had perceived it wrongly.

Like the blind scientist who described only one part of the size and shape of the elephant, this chapter also describes only one part of a much bigger and richer performance picture, your mental skills. Music performance is the culmination of the: mental, emotional, physical, technical, and musical aspects developed in practice and that come together during performance. If you are to continue to grow as a musician then you must embrace this performance elephant in its entirety. Understanding music performance from a purely technical and musical perspective is making the same mistake as the blind scientists. These are just part of a much larger performance picture. Developing and refining your mental performance skills is critical to sustaining high levels of performance. Incorporating mental skills into your total development as a musician will make your practices more effective and your performances more expressive while helping you to become a more confident musician.

The purpose of this chapter is to provide you with a broader understanding of the mental and emotional aspects of your performance. Although the mental skills discussed in this chapter make up just one part of the whole picture, they are often the part least understood and yet may be the most important in playing your best when it counts. A mental skills model is presented as a conceptual framework from which to gain a greater understanding of the richness and complexity of the psychological aspects of music performance. This model serves as a guide for the development of the mental skills necessary for optimal performance and provides the foundation from which this book is organized.

MENTAL SKILLS MODEL

The Mental Skills Model illustrates the levels of mental skills, mental abilities and mental disciplines needed to trust what you have trained in order to play your best when it counts. Think of this model as a pyramid with each lower level providing the necessary foundation for the next higher level. The foundation of the pyramid consists of the mental disciplines necessary for developing mental skills and integrating them into your performances. These mental disciplines are: self-leadership, self-management and passionate commitment.

The second level consists of your mental abilities. While you already have many of these abilities (e.g., the ability to talk to yourself effectively, set and attain goals, focus and refocus your attention, use positive emotion, and relax certain muscles during performance), each of these abilities can be further refined and developed when practiced effectively. These mental abilities are used to enhance the mental skills of confidence, concentration and composure, making up the third level of the model.

Finally, the top level represents your mental performance goal: Trust. Trusting during performance what you have trained in practice frees you of cognitive interference allowing you to attend to the higher order aspects of your performance - the feeling and the emotion in the music. When you trust what you have trained you let go of the conscious controlling tendencies often reinforced during technique development and practice sessions. Trust is a learned skill that ultimately frees you from the sources of distractions and allows your system to process the necessary information in a rapid and accurate way. This book will help you develop the mental skills leading to greater confidence and trust during performances.

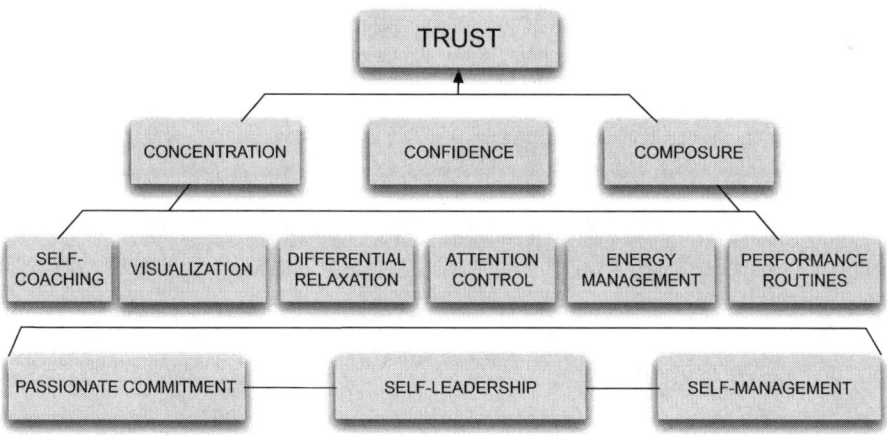

TRUSTING WHAT YOU HAVE TRAINED

The primary mental goal during your performance is to trust what you have trained. Trust involves freeing yourself of expectations, fears, or other cognitive activity and maintaining a clear and present focus during performance.

To fully understand trust as a specific performance goal it is sometimes helpful to separate it from the mental skill: Confidence. Confidence is a belief in something that is perceived to be known, such as, "I have confidence in my ability to play this piece of music." Confidence is also an expectation, such as, "I expect to play this piece well." Your confidence level results from the evaluation process of analyzing your current skill level and its relationship to the specific task demand. Trust, on the other hand, is a lack of analysis or expectation and exists in the moment without any past or future. Trust also implies a 'leap of faith' into the unknown. This is perhaps the most important and unique feature of trust. It is a conscious decision to let go of any conscious control and trust this will result in your best performance. Although confidence in your ability may affect the frequency with which you trust, the presence or absence of trust remains a conscious choice that is independent of internal and external factors.

MENTAL PERFORMANCE SKILLS

Your mental performance skills consist of: confidence, concentration, and composure. Although these skills can be trained separately, they are interrelated during your performances. For example, when you are confident, you focus your attention better which leads to being more relaxed. Being relaxed and focused increases your level of confidence.

Confidence

Confidence separates good performers from great performers. It is a belief or feeling of certainty you will successfully perform at a desired level. Most performers agree, of all the psychological skills, confidence has the greatest affect on performance. Not only is it the gateway to a trusting mindset but confidence also enhances the other mental and emotional processes needed to play your best. It has been said, "Becoming competent is an accomplishment, but becoming confident is a choice." Although this might be true, becoming confident may require a greater commitment to develop for some musicians than for others. However, choosing to think and act confidently, choosing to believe in yourself and choosing to proactively develop your confidence, is still a matter of your choice and your will to do so.

Concentration

Focusing correctly leads to greater confidence and higher levels of performance. Concentration is the process of consciously directing your focus, resulting in your enhanced ability to take in relevant cues necessary for skill execution. You can train your concentration muscle so you will focus attention more intensely and for longer periods of time but, please note: It takes training! The essence of optimal concentration during performance is learning to discern when you are distracted and having the skill and presence of mind to refocus. It is this *focus* and *refocus* repetition that builds task concentration, much like the work-rest ratios that build stronger, less fatigued muscles.

Composure

Composure is fundamental to performing your best under pressure. Composure is essentially the management of emotional energy. Just as positive emotion provides the energy that drives performance, negative emotions, such as; frustration, anger and fear drain your energy. Experiencing these negative emotions increases heart rate, muscle tension, constricts vision and ultimately cripples performance. When you master the skill of composure, bad things can happen, mistakes can occur, yet you can remain relaxed and focused. The capacity to mobilize positive emotional energy on demand is important for creating a positive performance mindset for your performance.

MENTAL ABILITIES

Mental abilities are often talked about in sport and performance psychology. While these abilities are important they are each only one piece of a larger, ongoing process aimed at optimal performance. The mental abilities introduced below will be sharpened throughout this book. As you harness the power of your mental abilities, you will learn how to better use them to enhance your confidence, concentration and composure.

Self-Coaching

Self-coaching is not to be confused with self-talk. Although they are similar, self-coaching is a much more purposeful inner dialogue. Self-coaching is the ability to give yourself what you need mentally and emotionally to stay confident and focused throughout a performance or during a practice session. Self-coaching is much more than just positive thinking. Just like a coach, there may be times when you need to think negatively or talk to yourself in a harsh tone to regain focus, overcome fear or correct a lackadaisical effort. However, more often than not, being a good self-coach involves *positive emotional coaching* that keeps you focused and fighting. To sustain a high level of effort during practice and belief during performance, you must develop and refine your ability to coach yourself.

Visualization

The ability to effectively use all your senses to vividly create, simulate or re-create various aspects of performance in your minds eye is called visualization. Visualization has been used by athletes, dancers, musicians, artists, and business professionals to positively affect their performance. You can use visualization to build quick, flawless pathways between the mind and body helping you perform complex movements without thinking. Visualization can also be used to enhance the feel of particular movements or to increase your ability to process performance cues more quickly and effortlessly. It can also be used to improve concentration, enhance confidence and better control how you respond emotionally to situations. You can also use visualization to speed learning. Your ability to create images in your mind is one of the greatest gifts you have been given. Learning to use it effectively is paramount to getting where you want to go as a performer.

Attention Control

Control over your attention or focus is at the core of your ability to deal effectively with the various distractions inherent present in practices, performances, and life. Attending to task relevant cues, maintaining focus for a time, and refocusing when necessary, are at the core of being a great performer. The ability to shift focus to selective aspects of performance is critical for processing the correct information at the optimal time. Attention control involves focusing on relevant cues that assist you in preparation, performance, and evaluation, without becoming preoccupied with the aspects of your environment or performance that are irrelevant, distracting, or over which you have no control.

Differential Relaxation

Differential relaxation is the ability to detect and release muscle tension in *specific* areas of your body. This is very different from what is typically understood as relaxation where your whole body is in a totally relaxed state. During performance, you rarely want your body to be completely relaxed but you do want certain muscles more relaxed than others. This is necessary to effectively and efficiently create skilled movement patterns. When playing a musical instrument you need more tension in your core muscles than in your hands and arms. The key is to recognize at which point your muscle tension begins to interfere with your performance. Once you recognize the interference, you need the ability to "release" the excessive tension and return to your optimal state of tension-relaxation.

Energy Management

The ability to create positive emotional energy on demand and to release negative emotional energy when necessary is at the heart of effective energy management. Most performances provide clear challenges to your ability to manage your emotions. This is especially true when performance outcome is the primary measure of success or failure. Management of this emotional energy requires you learn to pump-up when you are deflated and to calm-down when you are overexcited or nervous. Both require different management strategies. One of the keys to performing at peak levels is to learn how to create and maintain the correct amount of positive emotional energy regardless of your performance outcome.

Preparation Routines

Preparation routines are a pre-planned, structured sequence of thoughts and actions that act to get you mentally, physically and emotionally, ready to engage in a task, or help to organize your approach to a performance or event. For example, you might have a morning office routine where you look over what is on your schedule for the day, organize your thoughts and goals for your upcoming events (e.g., meetings, phone calls), tasks (e.g., reading a document, competing an assignment) or errands (e.g., picking up something in town). A pre-performance routine should include specific thoughts and actions preparing you to successfully execute the performance skill of trust or for creating a positive performance mindset immediately before going on stage. Although they are very individualized, performance routines will include similar aspects and should be practiced like other skills.

MENTAL DISCIPLINES

Mental disciplines provide the necessary support and energy to develop and refine your mental skills and abilities. These disciplines address the necessity to create a vision for success (self-leadership), develop a path to reach that vision (self-management), and the drive to sustain your efforts (passionate commitment). The disciplines of self-leadership and self-management are necessary to sustaining levels of high performance in the face of ever increasing pressures, distractions and rapid changes in your world. The discipline of passionate commitment address the laws governing personal development and the necessity to take responsibility for the growth and maintenance of your personal capacities.

Passionate Commitment

As was discussed in the previous chapter, committed, caring musicians are the ones who generate and deliver signature performances on a consistent basis. The passion you bring to what you do provides the positive energy necessary for sustaining excellence as a musician. A passionate attitude is what keeps you going in the face of challenges and adversity. Sustaining this attitude requires you to effectively manage and regularly draw upon both your physical and emotional energy. While your physical energy provides the fundamental source of energy throughout the day, it is your emotional energy, your "internal climate," that drives high-level practices and performances. Regularly engaging in activities that create optimism for what you are doing and increase your self-satisfaction is necessary for creating and maintaining your passionate commitment.

Self-Leadership

Great leadership starts with a goal or a vision. Weather you are leading yourself or leading others, you must first have a clear understanding of where you are going and why. This involves creating a long-term goal for yourself as a musician that is aligned with, and connected to, your personal core values. Knowing why your goal is important and what you must give up to achieve that goal (e.g., free time, late nights) are necessary to staying focused and determined when accomplishing challenging goals. Individuals in all performance domains who have sustained high levels of success have demonstrated the mental discipline found in self-leadership.

Self-Management

Self-leadership provides the vision and self-management produces the behaviors and actions necessary to accomplish that vision. Self-management is doing what it takes to get where you want to go. This involves the daily and weekly management of the direction and intensity of your efforts. It involves identifying, organizing and accomplishing small goals on the way to the big goals. It was once said, "You either take care of the little things or they will take care of you." This idea is at the heart of effective self-management.

The advantage of creating specific incremental steps, a path of small successes, that ultimately brings you to your goal has been demonstrated throughout your life. Tasks as simple as making a cup of coffee, or as complex as writing a research paper, or adding an addition onto a house all involve a sequence of steps that ultimately lead to the desired outcome.

CHECK UP FROM THE NECK UP

One of the best ways to understand your mental skills is to reflect upon how they have affected your practices and performances in the past. The Mental Skills Inventory (MSI) consists of a series of statements describing your beliefs, thoughts, and emotions in both practice and performance situations. Rate yourself using a scale of 1 to 4 based on how much the statement applies to you. The points on the scale are as follows:

1. If the statement does not represent how you think or feel, circle "not me."
2. If the statement mildly suggests how you think or feel, circle "somewhat like me."
3. If the statement commonly reflects how you think or feel, circle "often like me."
4. If the statement represents an ongoing state of how you think or feel, circle, "Just like me."

As you go through the inventory you will find it helpful to mark those questions that are most meaningful or represent an area of immediate concern. You may also choose to make notes in the margins to maximize your learning. Once you have identified these areas you can begin to monitor your improvement using your High-performance Journal.

Mental Skills Inventory

Preparation Routines	1	2	3	4
1	I feel mentally and emotionally prepared for each performance.	Not me	Somewhat like me	Often like me	Just like me
2	I can easily adjust to pre-performance changes.	Not me	Somewhat like me	Often like me	Just like me
3	Before a performance, I feel more excitement than distress about performing.	Not me	Somewhat like me	Often like me	Just like me
4	I have an effective routine I use to prepare for performances.	Not me	Somewhat like me	Often like me	Just like me
5	I practice my pre-performance routine.	Not me	Somewhat like me	Often like me	Just like me

Passionate Commitment	1	2	3	4
6	I achieve the goals I set for myself.	Not me	Somewhat like me	Often like me	Just like me
7	I constantly look for opportunities to better my performances.	Not me	Somewhat like me	Often like me	Just like me
8	I enjoy getting the most out of my talents and skills.	Not me	Somewhat like me	Often like me	Just like me
9	I get enjoyment from pursuing my dream goal.	Not me	Somewhat like me	Often like me	Just like me
10	I am committed to being the best I can be.	Not me	Somewhat like me	Often like me	Just like me

Energy Management	1	2	3	4
11	Unexpected situations do not throw me off my game at all.	Not me	Somewhat like me	Often like me	Just like me
12	I am able to maintain positive energy after making a mistake.	Not me	Somewhat like me	Often like me	Just like me
13	When things are going badly, I can quickly calm myself.	Not me	Somewhat like me	Often like me	Just like me
14	I am able to keep my negative emotions in check.	Not me	Somewhat like me	Often like me	Just like me
15	I can create a positive performance mindset on demand.	Not me	Somewhat like me	Often like me	Just like me

Differential Relaxation	1	2	3	4
16	I regularly attend to my breathing as a way of releasing tension.	Not me	Somewhat like me	Often like me	Just like me
17	I can quickly calm myself when I become over anxious.	Not me	Somewhat like me	Often like me	Just like me
18	I am able to detect and release muscle tension when I need to.	Not me	Somewhat like me	Often like me	Just like me
19	I rarely find myself too tense during a performance.	Not me	Somewhat like me	Often like me	Just like me
20	I regularly practice relaxation exercises.	Not me	Somewhat like me	Often like me	Just like me

	Attention Control	1	2	3	4
21	Distracting thoughts rarely interfere with my performance.	Not me	Somewhat like me	Often like me	Just like me
22	I easily direct my attention on what I need to play my best.	Not me	Somewhat like me	Often like me	Just like me
23	I don't let my mind wonder to irrelevant things during performance.	Not me	Somewhat like me	Often like me	Just like me
24	I am able to refocus to the task at hand whenever I need to.	Not me	Somewhat like me	Often like me	Just like me
25	I am proud of my ability to stay focused during my performances.	Not me	Somewhat like me	Often like me	Just like me
	Self-coaching	1	2	3	4
26	I am confident in my ability to perform under pressure.	Not me	Somewhat like me	Often like me	Just like me
27	I project a confident, positive image during performance.	Not me	Somewhat like me	Often like me	Just like me
28	I often talk to myself in a way that helps me stay confident	Not me	Somewhat like me	Often like me	Just like me
29	I have a strong positive belief in myself and what I can accomplish.	Not me	Somewhat like me	Often like me	Just like me
30	I am rarely self-critical during my performances.	Not me	Somewhat like me	Often like me	Just like me

Visualization	1	2	3	4
31	I regularly create vivid images of myself performing great.	Not me	Somewhat like me	Often like me	Just like me
32	I am able to hear the correct sound before I play a note.	Not me	Somewhat like me	Often like me	Just like me
33	I can easily visualize the feel of desired movement patterns.	Not me	Somewhat like me	Often like me	Just like me
34	I visualize playing in the performance venue before I arrive on site.	Not me	Somewhat like me	Often like me	Just like me
35	I have good control over the images that come into my mind.	Not me	Somewhat like me	Often like me	Just like me

Trust	1	2	3	4
36	I often let go of conscious control when performing.	Not me	Somewhat like me	Often like me	Just like me
37	I free myself of concerns about being correct and not making mistakes during performance.	Not me	Somewhat like me	Often like me	Just like me
38	I often find myself completely absorbed in the moment.	Not me	Somewhat like me	Often like me	Just like me
39	I trust my skills and rarely think about them while playing.	Not me	Somewhat like me	Often like me	Just like me
40	I allow myself to play instinctively and musically.	Not me	Somewhat like me	Often like me	Just like me

	Self-leadership	1	2	3	4
41	I have a high degree of clarity in long-term goal as a musician.	Not me	Somewhat like me	Often like me	Just like me
42	I have a sense of direction and purpose as a musician.	Not me	Somewhat like me	Often like me	Just like me
43	I regularly act in ways that are consistent with my core values.	Not me	Somewhat like me	Often like me	Just like me
44	I avoid most crises by being well prepared.	Not me	Somewhat like me	Often like me	Just like me
45	I take time to reflect upon my big picture goal.	Not me	Somewhat like me	Often like me	Just like me

	Self-management	1	2	3	4
46	I do a good job of using my time the way I planned.	Not me	Somewhat like me	Often like me	Just like me
47	There are very few areas of chaos in my life.	Not me	Somewhat like me	Often like me	Just like me
48	At the end of the day I feel satisfied with how I invested my energy.	Not me	Somewhat like me	Often like me	Just like me
49	I effectively prioritize my daily tasks.	Not me	Somewhat like me	Often like me	Just like me
50	I make time during the week for things that are important to me.	Not me	Somewhat like me	Often like me	Just like me

MSI SELF-RATING SCALE

Instructions: The MSI is a self-assessment of many of the mental skills addressed in this book. Determine the total score for each the MSI categories and graph your scores. This provides a visual comparison of your mental skills.

MSI Categories

Preparation Routines (PR) _____   Self-Coaching (SC) _____

Passionate Commitment (PC) _____   Visualization (VZ) _____

Energy Management (EM) _____   Trust (TR) _____

Differential Relaxation (DR) _____   Self-Leadership (SL) _____

Attention Control (AT) _____   Self-Management (SM) _____

```
20
18
16
14
12
10
 8
 6
 4
 2
 0
    PR  PC  EM  DR  AC  SC  VZ  TR  SL  SM
```

POSTSCRIPT

One way to imagine how mental skills fit into your development as a musician is to visualize a spoked wheel rolling along a road full of speed bumps and potholes. The potholes and speed bumps represent the challenges you face as you develop and perform as a musician. These challenges test the strength of your spokes. In other words, you may have great technical and musical skills but, if your psychological skills are under developed, your wheel will get stuck and you will not play your best when it counts. Until you develop your psychological spokes, you will always play better during practices than you do during performances.

The hub of the wheel is your ability to trust during performance what you have trained in practice. This is the most important aspect of your performance. You can have great technique or superior talent, but if you don't trust it when it counts, you will not perform at the level you are capable. A trust mindset frees you from self-doubt and allows your performance to unfold automatically without conscious interference. To be a great performer, you will need to develop and refine all the spokes in your wheel.

SELF-REFLECTION QUESTIONS

1. Using the statements in the MSI determine your mental strengths and struggles. Review your responses to specific statements you rated high and low. Then write down the specific area represented by each statement indicating your strengths and struggles.

Mental Strengths

1. _____
2. _____
3. _____
4. _____

Mental Struggles

1. _____
2. _____
3. _____
4. _____

2. The statements you rate as "not me" deserve your priority attention. However, you may find some of these statements deserve more immediate attention than others since some of the statements you gave a lower rating may not currently represent a big problem for you. Nevertheless, they can describe a skill you want to improve. Pay particular attention to your three highest and three lowest mental skill categories. Then determine the three mental skills that, if improved, would make the greatest positive difference in your performance.

1. _____
2. _____
3. _____

3
Trusting What You Have Trained

The Fox and the Lion

A fox scurrying through the woods stopped short when he saw a lion coming down the same path from the opposite direction. Before his enemy could strike, the frightened fox bolted into the deeper forest. Stopping to catch his breath, the fox turned around anxiously to see if the lion was pursuing him. In fact, the King of Beasts had continued down the path, enjoying the fine day.

Sometime later, the fox and the lion met on the same path. But this time, the fox contained his fear and stepped aside to let the majestic beast pass.

"Good morning," the fox politely said.

"A good morning to you," replied the lion.

The third time the two met, the fox felt no fear, and he asked the lion about the health of his family.

Trusting your system to "get it right" without monitoring or controlling correctness can be very scary! In the parable of the Fox and the Lion, the fox feared the lion in their initial meeting, but through subsequent meetings, the fox contained her fear, stepped aside, and embraced the majesty of the lion. Similarly, as you practice trusting what you have trained, you will learn to contain your fears of letting go, appreciating the majesty of your mind/body system to get it right, you will embrace trust as your primary performance goal.

Whether you are a professional athlete, Wall Street trader, ballet dancer or musician, performing your best when it counts results from trusting your training and letting go of consciously controlling tendencies. When you truly trust, you let go of control over technical correctness and concern for making mistakes, allowing your performance to unfold automatically free from cognitive inference,. This enables you to fully express the feeling and emotion in the music. Trust is a skill that frees you from internal distractions and allows your system to process information in a rapid and accurate way.

One common misunderstanding held by musicians is the belief that they must wait until they are "good enough," their technique more refined or their music better learned, before they can trust what they have trained. If you wait until you think you are good enough, you will be waiting for a long time. How many musicians enter into a performance feeling totally prepared? For most musicians, there is always something that can be refined to make their performance better. Trusting what you *currently* have, although difficult and often scary, is your mental performance goal.

To become the best musican you can be, it is important for you to embark upon two parallel paths. These are; to continue to develop and refine your physical, technical and musical skills, and to train your ability to trust these skills during performance. Trust is a mental performance skill you can develop, refine and execute, just like any other skill. The goals of this chapter are to help you understand trust as a performance skill, teach you how to practice trust and help you execute trust during performance.

TRUST: A SPECIFIC PERFORMANCE SKILL

Much sport science research has been devoted to understanding how highly technical movement patterns are developed and refined through practice. Some of the mental skills identified as helpful during skill acquisition include: self-monitoring of correctness, analysis of cause and effect regarding movement outcomes, and self-instruction of correct movement patterns. Although these mental skills are helpful during the acquisition phase, they usually interfere with motor skill execution during performance, especially when under pressure. Performers in a variety of domains report that, during their best performances; they suspend all judgments about outcome, free themselves of expectations, fears, doubts, and other cognitive activity; and trust what they have trained. Think of the times in which you played your best. Chances are, your mind was quiet, there was little concern for correctness, you did not judge your mistakes and your focus was much more in the present than either the past or the future.

Letting Go of Conscious Control

Trust is defined as, "Letting go of the conscious controlling tendencies learned during skill acquisition and allowing the automatic processes, which have been developed through training, to run without interference." In short, it is your ability to let go of controlling the correctness of your technique and allowing your system, or body, to take over. This letting go of correctness is the central component of trust during performance and is sometimes referred to as "getting out of your own way."

To illustrate how conscious control can inhibit music performance, let's examine an everyday motor skill. Imagine the task of parking and getting out of your car. You have pulled into the parking space. Now, describe the sequence of body movements necessary to turn off and exit your car. Describe the proper movement sequence involving; your left hand, right hand, left foot, and right foot. You successfully complete this highly complex, precisely timed sequence of movements many times a day. Why is it difficult to consciously describe? Because you execute this movement pattern below conscious awareness and with little or no consideration of correct form or technique. You simply consider the successful outcome and make it happen with little conscious effort.

Imagine what would happen if we decided to video tape your getting-out-of-the-car motor program and showed you the "correct" movement sequences, explaining exactly how your arms, hands, feet, and legs moved and in what order. Then we put you back in your car and ask you to exit your car again, only this time using the "correct" movement sequence. We also administered a mild electric shock for out of sequence or incorrect movements. Now correctness really matters! To avoid the consequences of failure (i.e., being shocked) you would consciously try to control the correctness of your movements, making them slower, more effortful, and ultimately, less accurate. In this example, we took a complex motor pattern executed flawlessly below your conscious awareness, and by attaching a negative consequence to incorrect movements, brought these movements under conscious control and completely screwed them up. Sound familiar?

Many musicians are reluctant to truly embrace trust as a mental performance skill. One reason may be that most musicians have developed their skills in a culture emphasizing correctness and judging mistakes. Although your music development might be enhanced by such a self-critical eye, music performance is not.

Clear and Present Focus

Your best performances take place when your mind is clear and present focused. In the quote below, D.T. Suzuki suggests you play your best when you are "not calculating and thinking." Similar to a child, you are playing with a natural connection to your music, free to express and to explore.

"Man is a thinking reed, but his great works are done when he is not calculating and thinking. Childlikeness has to be restored with long years of training in the art of self-forgetfulness. When this is attained, man thinks yet he does not think."

... D.T. Suzuki

According to Suzuki, learning to perform in a childlike state, where you are trusting what you have without self-instructing or self-monitoring, takes training. When this childlike state or trusting mindset is attained during performance, "Man thinks yet he does not think." In other words, when your mind is clear and you are focused only on the task at hand, you are processing large amounts of information below conscious awareness and with little conscious thought.

If we go back to the example of getting out of your car, your system is processing large amounts of information automatically, without having to "think" about what you are doing. This type of information processing is a different type of thinking from the conscious thinking you do when you are solving a problem. Your system is solving the problem of getting out of your car without you having to consciously think about the solution. In other words, when you are playing your best, your system is automatically *thinking* during your performance. Your mind is clear and your system is processing the information automatically without cognitive interference regarding the correctness of your technique or the consequences of missing a note.

THE INNER GAME

In his book *Inner Game of Tennis*, Tim Gallwey first identified the conscious mind and subconscious mind as Self-1 and Self-2. The conscious mind, Self-1, is the "Thinker." It is the part of you that analyzes, self-instructs, self-monitors, and tends to get overactive when you have doubts, fears and anxiety during performance or practice. Self-2 is the "Doer." Self-2 is best understood as your motor control system that selects and executes programs from memory which are "run" during performance. Self-2 has no capacity to judge your actions as good or bad, or to fear any consequences of mistakes. When you are playing your best, Self-1 is quiet and trusts Self-2 to execute the correct movement patterns without getting in the way.

An example of the way these two selves work together is evident when driving your car home from work and missing your turn-off because you were thinking about a problem that occurred hours earlier. In this example, Self-1 was engaged in solving the work problem while Self-2 was driving the car. Your conscious focus was on the various issues surrounding the problem and possible solutions while your subconscious was simultaneously processing the information needed to drive your car successfully. In essence, Self-2 was driving the car and could continue to drive the car until you recognized you missed your turn, or if red brake lights flashed on the car ahead of you, or the stop light ahead turned yellow. In each case, Self-1 reengages and you now become consciously aware of driving your car.

Similar to playing music, driving your car is an example of a fairly automated skill that can be completed with only intermittent involvement by the conscious mind. As a musician, you will find it helpful to have a better understanding of the roles Self-1 and Self-2 play during your performances.

Understanding Self-1

Both Self-1 and Self-2 are essentially information processing systems. Self-1 is the conscious mind which is a serial processor, meaning it can only process information one bit and a time. For example, you cannot read a book and listen to music simultaneously. You are either consciously attending to the meaning of the words on the page or you are not. However, you may intermittently switch back and forth giving you the illusion of reading and listening at the same time.

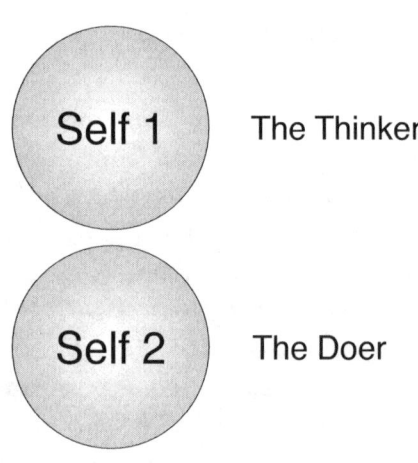

Self-1 processes information slowly and with conscious effort. Therefore, it rarely has a positive effect *during* the execution of complex motor patterns which require rapid and effortless processing. Self-1, your conscious mind, does not have the capacity to process the thousands of bits of information needed to perform the kind of movement patterns involved in most complex, automated skills found in music performance. In other words, trying to play a sonata on a piano using only Self-1 is analogous to trying to run the space station with an Apple 2e computer. It just cannot be done.

Because of Self-1's natural desire to control correctness, it is challenging to quiet Self-1 and trust Self-2.

Understanding Self-2

Self-2 is understood as a motor-control system operating below conscious awareness. It consists primarily of the interaction between the brain structures known as the Cerebellum, Cerebral Cortex, and Basal Ganglia. These structures allow you to carry out complex movements without having to think about them. This is where motor programs are stored, not in muscles themselves. Muscles are fibers that simply contract and relax on command. They have no capacity to remember. All the information needed to produce muscle movements are stored in motor programs located in the brain.

The simplest way to understand how Self-2 produces these complex movements below conscious awareness is to view a specific motor program as being analogous to a music CD. A music CD contains stored information that, when played, results in the specific song you selected. It is the stored puzzle pieces of instruments and vocals that, when put together, render the song you recognize. Put another way, the music CD contains the specifications for each song, which indicate each specific piece of sound data and the sequence in which they will be played, allowing you to hear instruments and vocals in their correct order and intensity. Like a music CD, a motor program contains the response specifications for a specific movement pattern. These specifications indicate what muscles are to contract, the sequence with which they are to contract, and the timing and intensity of the contractions. Literally hundreds of thousands of bits of information!

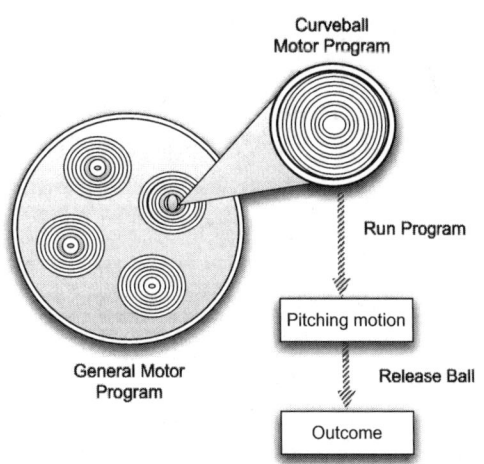

You have a number of well-learned motor programs stored in Self-2. For example, an accomplished baseball pitcher will have a motor program for the curve ball, the slider and the sinker. Although each pitch is a modification of the general "overhand throwing" motor program, they are still separate modifications resulting in a distinct motor program executed when the pitch is thrown. Similarly, a musician will modify existing programs to accomplish the goals required to perform a particular piece of music. This selection, modification, and execution of motor programs is best completed with very little conscious activity or Self-1 involvement. However, when the consequences for making mistakes increase, Self-1's desire to be correct also increases. This is why it is much easier to accurately execute complex movement patterns when you do not care about making a mistake.

THE INNER BATTLE

The inner battle during performance can be boiled down to the simple fact that *Self-1 does not want to trust Self-2*. This does not mean Self-1 *will not* trust Self-2, only that it *does not want to*. Self-1, by its nature, is a control freak. What this means is that Self-1 has no problem getting out of the way and trusting Self-2 as long as you do not care what happens. When you start to care about being correct or not making a mistake, Self-1 becomes active and tries to take control to get it right. When this happens, trust in self-2 breaks down.

Breakdowns in trust can occur at two different times: During the selection of the motor program from memory and during the execution of the motor program. Poor motor program selection often results from excessive cognitive activity, which impairs cue attenuation and prevents clear information processing. For example, the golfer who over-thinks, trying to recall the instructions for hitting the shot correctly, will rarely produce a good swing. Thinking too much impairs your system's ability to process relevant, meaningful cues necessary to select a solid motor program from memory.

During motor program execution, other breakdowns occur not as a result of inaccurate information, but due to conscious interference. Consider the pianist who enters into a difficult passage during performance and becomes excessively concerned with movement accuracy and fearful of making a mistake. Due to her concerns, she over-controls her movements, causing muscle tension, which then leads to incorrect movement patterns. In this example, she had selected a good motor program but got in the way of its execution by trying to over-control the correctness of her technique.

Trust can breakdown in four ways: jamming (over-thinking), over-aiming, pressing (over-trying), and over-controlling. If you truly trust your technique, you would not think too much, try harder than necessary, or over-control the correctness of your technique.

Jamming

This breakdown in trust is due to excessive cognitive activity either during motor program selection or during program execution. Jamming often occurs when you are over-instructing or over-analyzing either immediately before executing a movement pattern (reminding yourself of how best to move through an upcoming section of music that is technically difficult) or during the execution of a movement pattern (thinking about the correctness of your technique). Unfortunately, excessive cognitive activity does not *always* lead to poor performance outcomes. For example, there were times you have played well during practice and during performance while thinking too much. If you made a mistake every time you thought too much, you would quickly learn how to quiet your conscious mind. However, since you can often get away with thinking too much (especially during practice where you have multiple opportunities to execute the same movement pattern), you may never quite learn how to quiet your conscious mind effectively.

To better understand why you occasionally perform well while over-thinking, consider the analogy of listening to a familiar song on a poorly tuned radio. Although static may jam the reception and prevent you from hearing the song clearly, because you already know the song, you can "connect the dots" and still sing along. The same is true with familiar motor patterns. Occasionally, your system can overcome the static presented by over thinking and still execute the correct technical movement pattern. However, this does not happen often, and it is impossible to predict when it will happen. Your system's inability to overcome static becomes more evident when the static gets too loud. Even with well-learned movement patterns, too much thinking will jam the system. Jamming, or excessive cognitive activity, is often a result of anxiety, fear, or doubt. Sometimes poor execution caused by jamming is referred to as "paralysis by analysis."

Over-Aiming

Over-aiming occurs when you become excessively concerned with the accuracy of a movement. Focusing too much on the outcome heightens your muscle tension, resulting in an alteration of the movement sequencing. This is most commonly experienced in situations where mistakes are costly. For example, consider a percussionist reaching for a far note on the marimba and over aims, resulting in a slower, off rhythm strike. Once the percussionist becomes excessively concerned with accuracy, his vision narrows and he is unable to relax and trust his reach. His over-aiming prevents him from processing valuable information regarding the speed, angle, and trajectory necessary to play the note correctly.

Pressing

Pressing results from a perceived need to generate more force in the movement pattern. Pressing is often experienced when you attempt to try harder or to generate more speed or power. You probably can recall situations where you tried too hard or pressed, resulting in movement alterations. This is especially true during movement patterns where you feel you need to create excessive speed to produce the desired outcome. If you truly trusted your movements, you wouldn't press; instead, you would relax and let your system create the proper speed and force.

Over-Controlling

Over-controlling, or guiding the correctness of movement patterns, is also considered a breakdown in trust. This breakdown often occurs during movements that require a great deal of kinetic feel to execute properly. For example, when a golfer is hitting a lofted wedge over a green side bunker, the tendency is to over-control the correctness of the swing, often resulting in a loss of feel and a deceleration of the club head.

Whenever you consciously release control over correctness, you are taking a leap of faith. This is particularly difficult when you really care about not making mistakes. You honestly do not know if your fingers are going to do exactly what you want them to when you are playing. However, the more well-learned your movement patterns, the more likely things will work out as you have planned. Nevertheless, there still remains an unknown at the moment you initiate your movement. Picture a leap of faith as literally jumping over a crevice without knowing for sure if you will land safely on the other side. If you have cleared the crevice successfully in the past, then you have some degree of faith that you can and will do it again. You can trust if you commit to jumping and leaving the ground, you will succeed. This committed leap of faith is at the heart of trust as a performance skill. This leap requires an honest commitment to trust, if you let go, you are giving yourself the best opportunity to perform well. Without an unwavering commitment to trust, you will rarely land safely on the other side.

Understanding how and when trust breaks down during performance is a fundamental aspect of its development and refinement. Monitoring breakdowns in trust enables you to better understand the way trust is affected during various performance situations resulting in your ability to make corrections when necessary.

As mentioned before, if you truly trust, you will not think too much, try too hard, or over-control the correctness of your technique. You will find it helpful to recognize under what conditions you are most likely to exhibit each of the trust breakdowns. For example, you may try too hard on sections that require fast fingering, over-control during technically demanding sections, or think too much during melodic sections. Once you have a clear understanding of your natural tendencies or trust breakdowns, you can begin to address them during practice.

Breakdown	Example	Result
Jamming	Too many thoughts about the music, audience and the performance	1. Increased negative thinking 2. Broad attentional focus 3. Increased mistakes
Over-aiming	Large leap in the music, excessively concerned with accuracy	1. Doubt of making correct leap 2. Too narrow attentional focus 3. Excessive muscle tension
Pressing	Fast and loud section, perceived need to generate more force	1. Racing thoughts 2. Increased sense of urgency 3. Over played (too fast & loud)
Over-controlling	Playing a technically difficult passage, guiding the correctness of movement	1. Fear of making mistakes 2. Focus too narrow 3. Increased muscle tension

LEVELS OF SELF-BELIEF

To fully understand trust as a mental performance skill, you must understand its relationship to your perception of yourself as a musician and your belief in your capabilities. Although each of these levels of self-belief are somewhat interrelated, they differ in important ways. Your *self-concept* consists of your understanding and recognition of the personal characteristics you bring to your craft. You may believe yourself to be a more technical musician than a musical or expressive musician. You may also believe that your self-discipline and high achieving characteristics make you an effective practicer.

Your *confidence* is a belief resulting primarily from a self-evaluation of your capabilities and their relationship to the current performance demands. In other words, you may be more confident in playing technical pieces than you are expressive ones. However, having a high level of confidence does not mean you will perform successfully, but rather, you expect to be successful based on your belief in your current ability and your evaluation of the task difficulty. Although, your ability to *trust* can be affected by both your self-concept and confidence, whether you trust and let go of conscious control in the present moment, does not have to be determined by your self belief levels.

Performer Self-Concept

What do you believe about yourself as a musician? Your self-concept as a musician is a global belief about who you are and encompasses a broad range of personal characteristics and perceptions that have developed over time. In other words, your performer self-concept is the answer you come up with when you ask yourself, "*What are the personal characteristics that make up who I am as a musician?*" If you consider yourself to be hardworking, organized, and task oriented, chances are you have had this belief for many years. You will also most likely continue to believe these things about yourself as these characteristic express themselves during your development as a musician.

Your performer self-concept is important because affects what you believe is possible for you as a musician. If your perception of yourself as a musicians does not include the belicf that you have what it takes to succeed as a professional musician, then you most likely will not succeed. Most limitations we experience in our lives are the ones we place on ourselves and often stem from what we believe is possible based on our self-concept. You may believe you do not perform well under pressure and therefore become over anxious and negative before important events, or believe you are not good in math and avoid opportunities to develop this skill. In the book, *Psycho-*

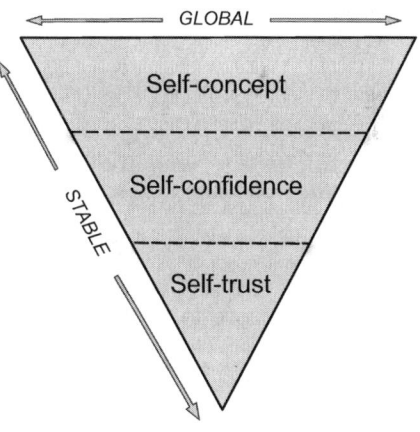

Cybernetics, Maxwell Maltz talks about his experiences as a plastic surgeon doing reconstructive facial surgery in the 1950's. He noticed a distinct difference in his patients' self-concepts following surgery. As a result of seeing themselves more positively (i.e., higher self-concept), his patients expanded what he called "the area of the possible." He goes on to suggest ways to expand what you believe is possible by changing your self-concept.

Performer Self-Confidence

Your self-confidence as a musician is more specific than your self-concept in that it includes a perception of value regarding your personal characteristics and performer competencies. In other words, your performer confidence is the answer to the question, *"Do I have what it takes to produce the outcomes I desire as a musician?"* To answer this question you must draw a conclusion as to your belief in yourself and your capabilities. This ultimately informs your expectation for success. If you are high in self-confidence you bring a level of expectation for success to the current performance. This expectation for successes is based on specific sources of information. These include, your past performance successes, other successful musicians with similar characteristics, positive comments from others whose opinion you value, and your perception of your ability to meet the current situational challenges.

Although the level of belief in yourself as a performer primarily results from an evaluation of these information sources, your expectation for success is more specific to the immediate task. An example of the specificity of confidence might be having a high expectation for success when speaking in front of a large group of people, but having a low expectation for success when hitting a drive off the first tee box at your local golf course. This task specific aspect of confidence adds to the instability of your performer self-confidence which makes controlling your thoughts and images all the more important. You may have a section in your performance where you tend to get stuck and lack confidence in your ability to execute successfully when the time comes. You still may be a confident musician, but one who has lost confidence in a specific aspect of your performance.

Performer Self-Trust

Performer self-trust is specific to the task at hand and specific to the moment of skill execution. Trust is not a continual state of mind and is very unstable during a performance. It is the instability and specificity of trust that makes it such a challenge to master. Although the levels of self-belief are somewhat interrelated to each other, they are still separate and distinct from trust. Even though a high expectation for success in executing a specific skill enhances the likelihood that you will trust it, that belief or expectation does not guarantee you will.

Unlike confidence, trust is the absence of all expectation regarding your ability or the outcome. Trust is the decision to let go of conscious control over correctness at the moment you are playing. Trust does not involve an expectation of a successful outcome. Granted, it is often easier to trust when you are confident, but being confident does not guarantee you will trust at the moment of skill execution. Trusting a specific movement pattern is still a separate and distinct skill that must be accomplished in the moment irrespective of your belief, your expectation for success, or the present conditions.

PERSONALITY AND TRUST

From my experiences working with performers in a variety of domains, I have found some individuals to have a greater disposition to trust during performance than others and this difference is due primarily to personality characteristics. The differences in the ability to trust can be explained when trust is viewed as having both a *State* and a *Trait* characteristic. We have discussed the State aspect of trust evident in skill execution during performance. *State Trust* is the act of letting go of conscious control within the present moment or current state. By contrast, *Trait Trust* is a personal predisposition to trust, or not trust, due to ones "hardwiring" or personal traits. For example, a musician who is high in creative, risk taking, and spontaneous traits is often high in Trait Trust. In essence, they are 'swimming down stream' when letting go and trusting what they have trained. On the other hand, a musician with perfectionistic characteristics, a strong desire to please others, and a more diligent and methodical approach to tasks, may be predisposed to a lower Trait Trust. Low Trait Trust individuals find it more difficult to let go. They are swimming up stream in their attempt to trust what they have trained.

Being predisposed to certain personality traits working for, or against, your ability to trust does not mean you will experience these characteristics to their fullest or be limited by their presence. As with other personality characteristics, Trait Trust involves a predisposition, or a natural bend, that can either be developed into a strength or overcome. For example, you may be highly introverted, but you have learned to overcome this personality trait when engaging in a professional meeting. The same is true in performance. Musicians that possess strong perfectionistic and over-controlling tendencies are able to learn to release control over technical correctness and trust during performance. The majority of this book is dedicated to helping you learn how to access State Trust regardless of your predisposition or Trait Trust. The interaction between Trait and State Trust can be better understood when describing four different personality profiles: The Perfectionist, The Performer, The Under-performer and The Artist, as seen in the diagram below.

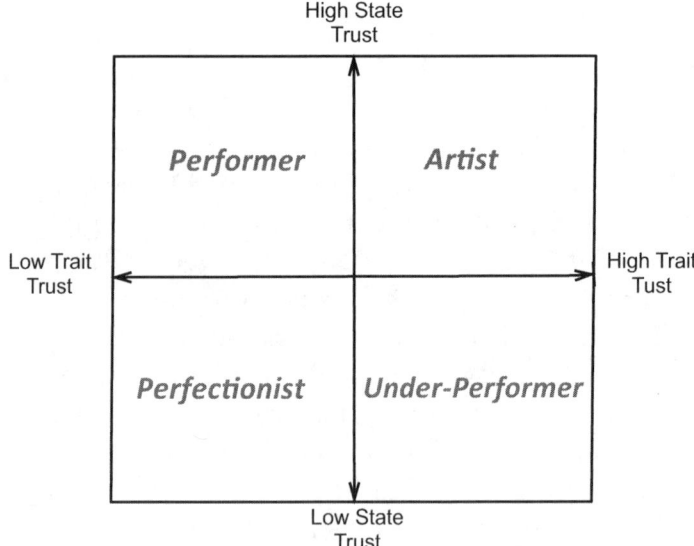

The Perfectionist

Perfectionistic personalities seem to be attracted to performance cultures that are technically demanding and place a high premium on correctness. Examples of these cultures include, gymnastics, piano, golf, and tennis. The Perfectionist is the person who likes doing things well and welcomes the challenge of working hard to get something "just right." She values correctness in the things she does, is typically driven and overachieving, and is often the person who comes to practice early and stays late.

Perfectionists are often understood by teachers and coaches as having a great attitude toward their development, are very coachable, and are typically great practicers. Their perfectionist tendencies keep them working very hard during practice; however, their self-critical nature and their strong desire for correctness often works against them during performance. Musicians who are perfectionistic can be very competitive with their own high standards and measure success primarily by performance outcome and perceptions of others.

Although musicians who match these characteristics will struggle with developing trust, they can learn to trust more frequently during performance. Letting go of controlling correctness will be an inner battle that does not play to their strengths. The goal is to embrace trust as a performance skill they must practice. This is more difficult than it seems and involves eliminating monitoring of technical correctness and accepting mistakes.

The Performer

Most great athletes or musicians are low in Trait Trust, but are high in State Trust. Because of their low Trait Trust they have a predisposition to work hard in practice. Belief in their skills and capabilities is grounded in completing quality repetitions and recognizing there are no short cuts to getting better. The Performer personality is also very purposeful in preparation leading up to performances. Although they are well grounded in structured practice sessions, they are open to, and regularly looking for, strategies, technologies, and methods to gain an edge on their competition or perform better.

Musicians who fit this profile love to challenge themselves and work hard at being the best. They perceive their mental skills as a strength and regularly lean into pressure as a way of testing these skills. The high State Trust characteristic frees them up to do whatever it takes to perform well without dwelling too much on mistakes, or shortcomings, before and during performances.

The goal for these musicians is to continue to embrace their musical and technical strengths. In highly technical tasks, accepting bad outcomes and moving on during performance can sometimes be a struggle that interferes with their ability to trust on a more regular basis.

The Artist

This personality type is high in both Trait and State Trust. They trust very easily in their abilities but also tend to overestimate their level of preparation for important events. This person is creative and freewheeling and can bore easily in practice sessions. They also have trouble sticking to a game plan during performances. However, when confident, they tend to perform very well.

It is not unusual for performers who fit this profile to be very talented. Being gifted in a particular area is often like being given too much money without having to work for it. Especially for musicians, when success comes too easily, it can often spoil their work ethic. Consequently, their confidence and their will to persevere are easily shaken whenever performance outcomes decline. Therefore, it is very difficult for these individuals to sustain trust over time and throughout difficult situations. They will rely primarily on their talent while continuing to experience inconsistent results in their performances.

The goal for the Artist is to accept the challenge of executing the correct process both in practice and during performance. If there is anyone who needs to make the process the product, it is the Artist profile. The problem is that they believe they can produce the desired outcomes without the correct processes, which is somewhat consistent with their past performance experiences. They will struggle when introduced to performance demands at the next level, where most musicians are of equal talent, and correct processes are at a premium.

The Under-Performer

The under-performer is often seen as an immature musician who does not put in the practice time necessary to perform at the level of their own expectations. A high level of Trait Trust often prevents him from putting "hay in the barn" during practice sessions. Musicians with this personality type sometimes learn things quickly and may be considered talented but underachieving. They easily become negative during performances and find themselves blowing off the pressure of the situation by using excuses. A fear of failure is sometime present with these individuals because of their overinflated view of their ability to perform.

The goal for the under-performer is to redefine the battle during performance by accepting the mental and emotional challenge of playing well. The battle to win lies within the processes of preparation and mental skills execution during performance, not winning the performance outcome. In other words, take control over what can be controlled and keep fighting a good fight.

TRUST DURING PERFORMANCE

Trust during performance is primarily a concentration skill that involves holding your attention in the present moment during a specific sequence of movements. Your capacity to trust, and ultimately to perform at your highest potential, is in direct proportion to the stillness of your mind. When your mind is noisy, anxious or distracted, it interferes with the processing of information necessary for skilled performance. When you increase your concentration capacity, you are, in essence, improving your ability to clear your mind of distracting thoughts more effectively and efficiently.

It is very difficult to "not think" for an extended period of time. Although, a trust focus involves a quiet conscious mind, you are still focused, but not thinking. Therefore, instead of trying to stop thinking as a way of developing a trust focus, you must put your conscious mind where it "thinks" in ways other than in words yet is meaningful to your performance outcome. As a musician, you can choose to attend only to listening to the sound you are making. If you do this for ten minutes, directing your attention back to listening periodically as it drifts off to other things (e.g., self-instructing, monitoring mistakes), you will build your ability to quiet your conscious mind and trust what you have trained. The idea behind building a trust focus is your conscious mind (Self-1) will go where it is most comfortable, thinking and analyzing, unless you direct it somewhere else. As a rule, if you don't control Self-1, it will control you.

When you find yourself thinking in words during a performance, you are not in a trusting mindset. Therefore, you must consciously put your focus in a place where it will help you the most. The more vivid your images and sensations the easier it is to stop thinking in words. Many musicians inadvertently train themselves to think in words during practice sessions by self-critiquing their practice repetitions (e.g., self-instruction, analysis of cause and effect). This usually occurs before, during, or after movement patterns you are working to improve or refine, engraining the habit of thinking during performance. Although this type of self-critiquing is often necessary and beneficial, it can become a negative habit that interferes with your ability to clear your mind and trust during performance.

One of the obstacles you face in moving from skill development to skill performance is the tendency to judge aspects of your performance as good or bad and classify your movement technique as right or wrong. This lack of acceptance during performance results in excessive thinking and analyzing. Letting go of conscious control and quieting your mind begins with the practice of acceptance or nonjudgmental thinking. It is important for you to understand the relationship between a judgmental, non-accepting mindset and your inability to release conscious control over correctness. This is similar to having a judgmental parent standing over you while you are washing the dishes after dinner. Knowing that you are being judged on every move, you become conscious of making a mistake and therefore try to control correctness. Being too judgmental not only leads to more mistakes during performance but takes away from the enjoyment that is possible. The power of acceptance can be demonstrated in many areas of our lives but this is especially true during performance.

PRACTICING A TRUST FOCUS

I am a big believer in applying the 80-20 rule when practicing or developing trust as a performance skill. The 80-20 rule refers to the ratio of blocked to variable practice during a typical practice session with blocked practice being used for skill development and variable practice being used for training trust. Blocked practice occurs when you work on refining a specific movement pattern by completing a number of repetitions in a row while monitoring correctness. You may stop after a mistake midway through and start over or you might work on a particular sticking point until you get the sequence correct and start again at the beginning. In either case, you have identified a specific movement sequence, and are training this specific sequence through repetition. In other words, you have blocked a movement pattern that you are refining, to some degree, before moving onto another pattern. Blocked practice is necessary for motor skill development and the refinement of a specific motor program. However, when training trust, blocked practice is counterproductive and therefore variable practice is recommended.

Variable practice occurs when you change or vary the movement pattern from repetition to repetition. During variable practice, your motor system retrieves a program from memory, runs it during the first repetition, and then retrieves a different program for the next repetition. It is the retrieval of separate motor programs from repetition to repetition that makes this practice variable. Keep in mind, *retrieving a motor program from memory is a skill in and of itself*. If you do not practice retrieving motor programs, you will not get any better at it. That is one reason why variable practice is so important for the performance of technical movement patterns.

Variable practice allows for the opportunity to develop your ability to trust your movement patterns. One of the obstacles you face during blocked practice is the tendency to judge aspects of your movement patterns as correct or incorrect and classify your movement technique as right or wrong. This type of conscious activity (e.g., judging, instructing, analyzing) is often reinforced during blocked practice, especially in the early stages of the learning process. For highly technical activities involving professional instructors, it is not uncommon for musicians to practice primarily in a blocked format and become well-trained in over-analysis. Remember, letting go of conscious control, quieting your conscious mind, and trusting your motor pattern require the practice of nonjudgmental thinking.

Obviously, there are times when you will need to make judgments, monitor correctness and analyze technique in order to improve your skills, but you must also make time to quiet your conscious mind and practice your trust focus. The 80-20 rule implies during skill development and refinement, you should spend no more than 80 percent of your practice session in blocked practice and no less than 20 percent in variable practice. In so doing, you will ensure that you are spending time in each practice session developing both your performance skill, trust, as well as your physical and technical skills. However, as you get closer to a performance date and your skills are more well learned, you should slide this percentage more toward 80 percent variable practice and 20 percent blocked practice. The week before your performance you should practice at 80 percent variable and 20 percent blocked.

POSTSCRIPT

Trust, like other skills, must be trained in practice to be executed properly during performance. Training your ability to let go of conscious control and maintain a clear and present focus presents a different set of challenges during practice than training physical skills. If you were to ask most musicians, "What is the purpose of practice?" They would probably say, *"To make my technique better, more consistent and learn my performance piece."* Although this is certainly a noble challenge, it is not the same purpose as "to perform better." As we discussed, the psychological skills necessary for learning or putting it in the system are not the same skills as, and may actually *interfere* with, the skills needed to get it out of your system during performance.

Training trust must be done in practice and must be done with a total commitment to work solely on trust, excluding any technical or musical aspects of your performance. Therefore, time must be set aside during a typical practice session to work specifically on trust.

Making an honest commitment to training trust may not sound like a big step but it is one of the biggest! Trust is a difficult skill to train and requires harnessing your energy and focusing in a deliberate fashion. Once you have designated a specific time during your practice session to train trust, you must commit yourself to working only on that skill. You will find you will become easily distracted by technical mistakes and other competing demands while you are training trust. I will tell you now, you cannot learn to trust without an honest and complete commitment to focusing only on the development and refining of trust during its training. Embracing trust as a distinct performance skill requires a concentrated, committed effort in practice and is essential to its development.

Learning to trust requires distinguishing between the presence of trust and the absence of trust. Quieting the conscious mind, Self-1, is necessary for providing a reference point for the feeing of trust. Your capacity to trust is in direct proportion to the stillness of your mind. When your mind is noisy, anxious, or distracted, it interferes with the processing of information necessary for trusting your skilled performance.

Quieting the conscious mind and letting go of controlling tendencies can be very challenging for a number of reasons. Because the conscious mind is built to seek stimulation, complexity, and challenge, quieting your mind to focus on one thing is counter to your hardwiring. Therefore, a high degree of self-awareness and willpower is necessary to attaining your goals when training trust. A second reason trust is difficult to train is the developmental culture prevalent in most music schools. Typically, during a practice session, you spend a great deal of time thinking, monitoring, problem-solving, and analyzing to develop and refine your technical and musical skills. This type of practice is very different from what you will experience when training trust and you must resist the temptation to revert to this practice mindset when training trust.

SELF-REFLECTION QUESTIONS

1. How will trusting what I have trained affect my performance?

2. What are the barriers I perceive to implementing the 80-20 rule?

3. Am I willing to make an honest commitment to training trust?

4. Think about the relationship between your thinker (Self-1) and your creative and intuitive doer (self-2) during your performance (and even in other aspects of your life). Describe three situations when Self-1 has got in your way and prevented you from becoming absorbed in the present moment.

Situation 1:
Situation 2:
Situation 3:

1. Identify a situation for each of the breakdowns in trust and describe your response to that breakdown. Then write down your response and develop a correction for the next time it occurs. Example: 1. Situation: I run through a passage in my mind anticipating ways I could make a mistake, 2. Response: I start to panic, become tense and clinch my jaw. 3 Correction: Calmly sing the passage in my head. Take some deep breaths.

Break down	Situation	Response	Correction
Jamming			
Over-aiming			
Pressing			
Over-control			

1. Which of the four personality types best describes you? Why?

My personality profile is:

2. Provide examples of how you use variable practice.

1
2
3
4

4
Self-confidence From The Inside-Out

There is More Light Here

A man saw his friend searching for something on the ground, "What have you lost, Mulla?" he asked.

"My key," said the Mulla.

So the man went down on his knees too, and they both looked for it.

After a time, the other man asked: "Where exactly did you drop it?"

"In my house."

"Then why are you looking outside?"

"There is more light here than inside my house."

Where would you look if you wanted to become a more confident musician? Your past successes would have the most light. There is no doubt past success breeds confidence, but confidence does not necessarily result from either your competence as a musician, or your past successes. You probably know a musician who is good but lacks confidence and, you may know a musician who is not very good, yet has much confidence. If confidence was truly dependent on successful outcomes or how well one played, then good musicians would always be confident and bad musicians would always lack confidence. We know this is not true. Confidence in yourself as a musician and performer has more to do with what is inside: what you believe, how you think, and how you act, than what is outside - how well you perform.

Believe it or not, confident performers choose to be confident performers. They take control over their thoughts and images, before, during, and after performances. They create feelings of playing great and visualize themselves successfully executing under pressure. Inside you exists the tools necessary to become a more confident performer. It is simply a matter of whether you choose to use these tools or not. Using these tools correctly requires commitment and self-control. There are many forces acting to pull you into a negative, self-defeating state of mind. Making a commitment to stay positive, and exhibiting the self-control necessary to monitor and eliminate negative and self-defeating thoughts is fundamental to building your confidence.

Although becoming more confident may require a greater commitment from some musicians than others, choosing to believe in yourself, to think and act confidently, is still a matter of your will to do so. Where would you look for confidence if you were trying to find it? If you are like Mulla, you would look outside where there is the most light but, the key is on the inside.

CHOOSING TO BE CONFIDENT

Confidence is a *belief*. It is a belief in your capability to create a desired outcome. As a musician, being confident is believing you will hit your notes, express feeling and emotion in the music and connect with your audience. Like other beliefs, believing in your capabilities is a choice you make. However, many musicians believe their confidence is a reflection of external factors such as, recent successes, good practice sessions, or positive comments from instructors. They do not believe confidence is something they control. Some musicians even perceive positive thinking as a form of self-deception.

When your confidence is based on external factors or outcomes, your belief ebbs and flows with the ups and downs of your performance evaluations. When your confidence is based on internal factors or processes (thoughts, feelings, images), it is possible to feel confident despite unfavorable external factors. You choose what you believe, how and what you think, independent of the situation. Although you can work diligently on the various aspects of your performance, until you deeply and honestly believe you alone, controls the quality of your thoughts and images, your confidence will be dictated by external events.

Many people believe a confident mindset is what separates good performers from great performers. Although regardless of your current level, you will perform better with confidence than without it. When you ask musicians to describe what it is like to play with a confident mindset, they often talk about beliefs and feelings. For example,*"When I enter into a difficult passage, I feel like I know exactly where my fingers are going," "I feel like I can do no wrong,"* or *"I feel calm and in control of my emotions."* For most musicans, this translates into a feeling of certainty they will perform at their best. Confidence, like other beliefs and feelings, affects both your expectations and your interpretations of events. This is one reason why most performers agree of all the psychological skills, confidence has the greatest impact on their performance outcomes. Besides allowing you to trust what you have trained, confidence enhances the other mental and emotional processes needed to perform your best. Obviously, some musicians are able to prepare poorly and think ineffectively, yet still feel confident about a particular performance, and some need not practice much to perform well. However, the vast majority of musicians, creating a confident mindset that holds up across a variety of performance situations results from effective habits of thinking, feeling and visualizing.

TOOLS FOR BUILDING CONFIDENCE

Your self-confidence is built with three basic tools common to all human beings. These are; the ability to choose your thoughts and actions; the ability to be self-aware of thoughts, feelings and behaviors; and the ability to imagine beyond what exist in your present reality. These three tools can be used to empower each of us to fulfill our potential. Sometimes things may interfere with your ability to fully utilize these tools. Examples include, trauma, toxic relationships, poverty, illness or addiction. When your ability to use these basic human tools is compromised, it is critical to address the problem. Counseling is a very effective method for regaining full access and use of these tools. However, for most musicians, becoming a more confident performer is simply a matter of recognizing the power of these tools, how they are currently being used, and getting some assistance in using them more effectively. Below is a summary of the three tools for building confidence.

Freewill

Freewill is your ability to think and act, independent from other influences. Until you honestly believe you control how you approach situations, and how you respond to situations, you will never reach your potential as a performer. You are responsible for what goes through your own head. It is not the situation, your upbringing, or your genetics, that determine what you think or how you act. Your thoughts and actions are a function of your personal, independent freewill. You can create the mindset in which you perform your best. You can choose how you spend your time and energy. You can choose what you believe about yourself and your capabilities. It is up to you.

Musicians rarely have direct control over all that happens before, during, or after a performance. Music performance, like other performances in highly competitive or stressful environments, is more often about managing discomfort and adjusting to mistakes than it is about being comfortable and executing flawlessly. How you approach and how you respond to the unexpected, the negative and the positive events that surround your performance, is completely up to you. Becoming a confident performer results from proactively choosing your thoughts, images and behaviors in a ways that keep you positive and focused.

Self-awareness

Your ability to step outside yourself to examine and reflect upon your beliefs, actions or experiences, is the tool of self-awareness. Improvement in any aspects of your life, or your performance, is grounded in your ability to be self aware. To develop as a musician, you must not only become aware of your mental and emotional strengths and struggles, but you must also become aware of your mental and emotional patterns and their effect on your performances. Like physical habits, mental habits often unfold automatically and without conscious awareness. Having a keen awareness of what you are currently doing and what you would like to do is a necessary first step in developing a new habit or changing an old habit. Keep in mind, awareness is only the first step. Although self-awareness facilitates your ability examine your habits (in a brutally honest way), it is your freewill that enables you to change them.

You may currently have habits of approaching and responding to performance events in ways that create self-doubt, but you can change these habits and develop new, more effective habits, ones that instill and maintain your self-confidence. Awareness of your habits of thinking and responding is an important tool to help you play your best.

Imagination

How well you use your imagination is a primary factor in your success as a performer. Do not leave this tool in your tool box! Use it often and use it well. Your imagination enables you to create feelings, pictures, and thoughts outside your current reality. Whenever you think about a future performance or recall a past performance, you are using your imagination. Because your mind often does not distinguish between a vivid image and a real event, you can truly "make a heaven out of hell or a hell out of heaven." You are constantly using your imagination throughout the day so why not use it in ways that enhances your self-belief and programs your mind for success.

Confidence, like other beliefs, is formed by your imagination and interpretation of events. What you imagine before an upcoming performance affects how you feel about it, whether either excited and energized, or fearful and anxious. Additionally, the images you choose to recall following a performance provide a powerful source of information you store in memory and use to draw conclusions about your future capabilities. *Confident performers choose to visualize in ways that create feelings of certainty rather than doubt.* They consciously control their images before and after performances. Confident performers consistently create images of winning or executing flawlessly, reinforcing a positive belief in themselves and an expectation they will perform well.

TALKING TO YOURSELF

Have you ever stopped and listened to the way you talk to yourself throughout the day? What types of things do you say? What tone of voice do you use? When thinking about an upcoming practice session, a lesson with your instructor, or a studio class, do you talk to yourself in ways that energize you? How do you talk to yourself during a typical practice session? Do you have a habitual statement you say to yourself following a mistake? How do you respond after successfully executing a difficult section of music? Your inner dialogue has a great deal of influence over how you approach and respond to situations and what you believe is possible for you as a musician. It is advantageous to understand not only what you are saying to yourself, but when and how you are saying it.

Many musicians make the mistake of "going with the flow." That is, when things are going well they talk to themselves in positive ways and when things are going poorly they get frustrated and negative. It takes self-disciple to talk to yourself in ways that help you be positive, concentrative, and persistent when things are not going your way. Once you believe how and what you think is your choice and begin to take responsibility for it, you will gain greater influence over the energy, focus, and confidence you bring to your practice sessions, to your performances, and to other areas in your life. Accepting responsibility for your inner dialogue is the first step in gaining control over how you coach yourself.

Self-coaching

When musicians are having trouble with self-confidence, the first thing I want to know is how good of a coach they are to themselves. It is difficult to be a poor self-coach and maintain your confidence, enthusiasm and focus for an extended time. Choosing to be a good self-coach means making a commitment to stay focused and energized from the beginning to the end. Great self-coaching in practice and performance, as well as in life, may be one of those things that is hard to describe but we all know it when we experience it. Great self-coaches are people who consistently give themselves what they need, mentally, emotionally, and physically, to keep their attitude positive, mind focused, and their fighting spirit engaged.

How well do you coach yourself? On a scale of 1 to 10, with 10 being great, how would you rate your ability to give yourself what you need to stay positive and focused? If you read a transcript of your inner dialogue during a practice session, how would it read? After reading that transcript, would you feel better about yourself, or worse? Next time you practice, listen to what you say to yourself. Simply step outside yourself and listen to what you are saying, not making any judgments, or stopping any thoughts. Pay particular attention to any patterns of self-statements especially when responding to mistakes. Start this week. At the end of each practice, ask yourself, "If I printed a transcript of my self-coaching today, how would I rate it on a scale of 1 to 10?"

Body Language

A musician once told me whenever playing in front of his instructor he took special care not to physically react to mistakes occurring during his performance. He believed showing poor body language caused his instructor to become upset. However, when he played in front of his peers, he expressed his negative emotion and body language more often and he felt this hurt both his confidence and his performance. Once he became aware of the affect his body language had on his confidence, he decided he would, 'act as if' he was playing in front of his instructor even when he was not. This made a difference in his physical responses and self-confidence during performances. Simply acting confidently can lead to feeling and thinking confidently. Acting as if you are confident, walking with shoulders back and chin up, has positive affects on your thoughts and feelings. It can lift your attitude and spirit, especially during difficult times.

Take a moment and think about the characteristics you believe make a great self-coach. Reflect upon some of these characteristics and what it looks like, feels like, and sounds like when you are being a great self-coach.

Characteristics of a Great Self-coach
_____
_____
_____

YOUR THREE EGO STATES

In the early sixties, Eric Berne, M.D., wrote the book, "Games People Play" in which he talked about different ways we interact with others, specifically, the dialogue between two people - the social transaction. This book was part of an emerging field in psychology called Transactional Analysis (TA). TA suggested we all carry inside us three separate selves called "ego states": the Parent ego state, the Adult ego state, and the Child ego state. Each ego state has a different way of thinking, feeling, and believing. When you are talking from your *Parent* you may be either critical (*"Why do you keep making the same mistake?"*) or supportive (*"You can do this, try it again"*). When you are speaking from the *Adult* you are stating a rational observation without any judgements as to the correctness or whether it is good or bad. For example, *"You over reached on that last note,"* or *"This auditorium has lots of dead space."*

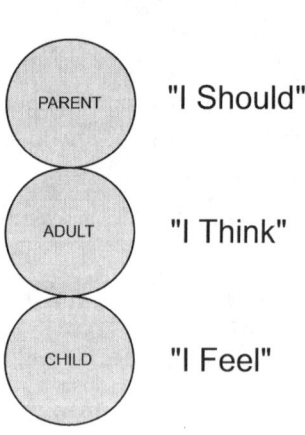

Your *Child* is the one that tries to please others, rebel against authority, or just have fun. It also responds emotionally to events and other people. Usually, when you are responding to another person or situation in a fearful, frustrating, or a joyful manner, you are doing so from your Child ego state.

Transactional Analysis uses the three ego states to analyze social transactions between two people based upon the ego state from which one person is speaking and the ego state from which the other person is responding. For example, you greet a coworker when passing them in the hallway with the phrase, "*How are you?*" and they respond, "*Fine, thanks, how are you?*" while you both smile and keep walking. This is considered to be a complementary Adult-to-Adult transaction. This

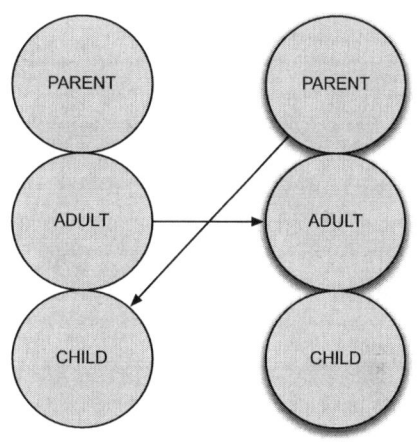

transaction becomes crossed if your coworker reponds by saying, "*I'm running late thanks to you! You shouldn't have talked so much in that meeting.*" In this example, instead of responding from the Adult, your coworker responded from their Parent and "hook" your Child in an attempt to make you feel guilty. According to Berne, this is when the game begins.

One way to better understand and change the way you talk to yourself is to apply the concept of the three ego states to your own internal transactions. You have an internal dialogue going on between your Parent, your Adult, and your Child throughout the day, as well as during your practices, and possibly your performances. For example, when you say to yourself, "*I can't believe you just made that mistake,*" who is "*I*" and who is "*You*" in this statement? By applying the theories of TA to your own internal transactions, you become more aware of your self-talk and how it affects your attitudes, behaviors and beliefs regarding your approach and response to various situations.

INTERNAL TRANSACTIONS

Think for a moment about the three ego states you carry around inside you. Now apply them to the inner conversations, or internal transactions, you have with yourself. Think of the different roles each of your ego states play when you talk to yourself. Your Parent may take on the role of the critical parent during a practice session, responding with negative or critical self-statements following your mistakes. Your Adult, on the other hand, is the rational self-observer, or instructor, who makes nonjudgemental observations or self-statements that might solve a musical or a technical problem.

Your Child may be the most complicated of the three ego states. Like the Parent and the Adult, the Child responds with self-statements and actions. However, unlike the other two ego states, the Child also reacts with feeling and emotion. This occurs when you emotionally respond to an event or situation with either positive feelings (e.g., smiles after executing a difficult musical section, fist pump when feeling a sense of accomplishment) or with negative feelings (e.g., becoming fearful when thinking about an upcoming performance, reacting with frustration or anger after repeated mistakes). There is also a part of your Child Ego State that is called your Natural Child. You experience your Natural Child when you are having fun and naturally connected to what you are doing in the moment. Think of a child playing in a sandbox being free, spontaneous, and creative without any concern for making mistakes or thoughts of being correct, and without any concern for what other people may be thinking. More than likely, it is within your Natural Child that your best performances lie.

Responding to Mistakes

To better understand how you talk to yourself from these ego states, think about how each might respond differently to the same situation. In other words, if you were repeatedly making the same mistake during a single practice session and you became angry or excessively frustrated, you would be responding from your Emotional Child (EC). If you were to stop after a couple of successive mistakes and implement a solution (e.g., taking a deep breath and then hearing the correct sequence and rhythms of sounds in your mind) before starting over, then you are responding from your Adult (A). When you are in your Supportive Parent (SP) you may respond with encouraging words such as, "*I know you can do this. Stay patient and relaxed and you will get it.*" When in your Critical Parent (CP) you might berate yourself, "*I am terrible! I should just quit! I will never get this right.*"

How might your Natural Child (NC) respond to making the same mistake when working through a difficult section of music during practice? Remember, your Natural Child's primary goal is to have fun. This means your Natural Child wants to keep playing and does not want to get bogged down by anything interrupting the fun and enjoyment of playing your instrument, especially boring repetitions. Your Natural Child would most likely respond by trying to complete the difficult section a couple of times and then move on to another more enjoyable aspect of practice.

You have well developed patterns of self-statements making up your habits of approaching and responding to situations. These self-statements arise from your ego states. The more developed a particular ego state, the more frequently you talk to yourself from that ego state. If you are self-critical during practices and following performances then you most likely have a highly developed Parent ego state. On the other hand, if you are less judgmental and more solution-oriented, you have a developed Adult ego state. If you are easily frustrated during practice, then your Emotional Child is very active.

Often, the activity level experienced in certain Ego States outside of practice is different from that during practice, but this is not always the case. For example, the inner dialogue for most musicians during practice tends to be more demanding and goal-directed, but the perfectionist, being overly self-critical and judgmental is a common inner dialogue outside of practice as well.

CHART YOUR INTERNAL DIALOGUE

In the graph below, chart the percentage of time you spend in each of the ego states during a typical day or practice session. The graph includes your Critical Parent (CP), Supportive Parent (SP), Adult (A), Emotional Child (EC) and your Natural Child (NC). The goal is to determine your natural self-coaching style (i.e., during a typical day) and your practice self-coach style (i.e., during a typical practice session). In this exercise think about the ways you are most of the time.

The graph below is an example of an individual's natural self-coaching (left bar) and her practice self-coaching during a typical practice session (right bar). Chart your own inner dialogue using this example as a guide.

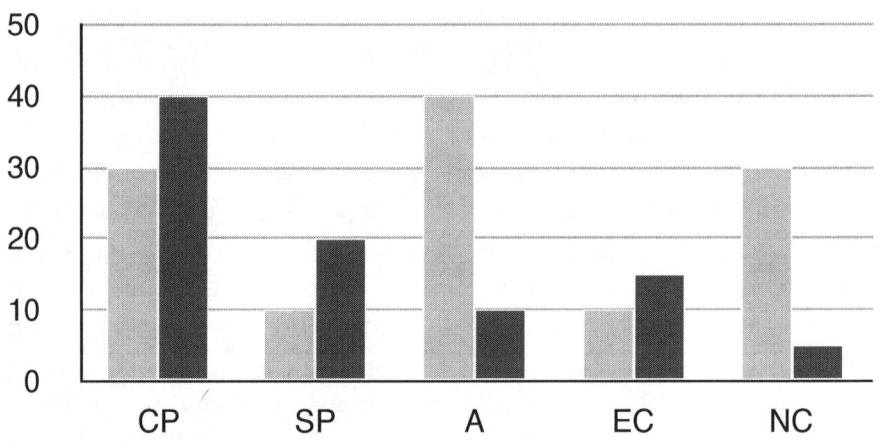

My Inner Dialogue

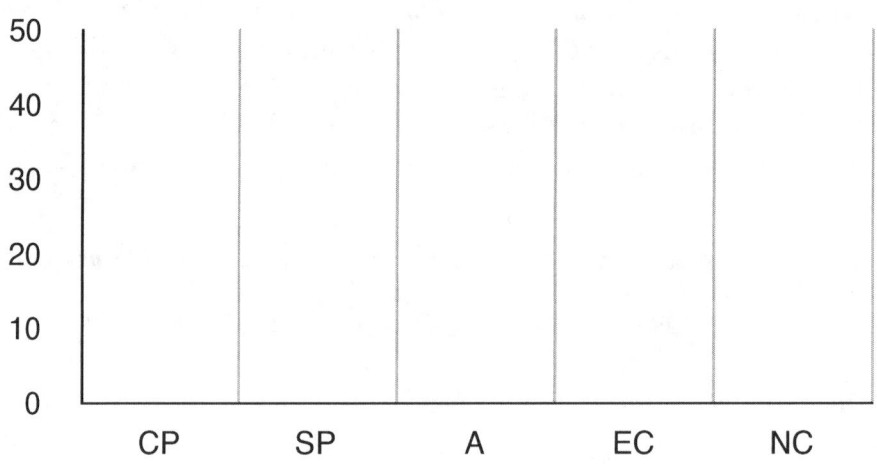

PERFECTIONIST SELF-TALK

One of the most interesting aspects of working with performers in both athletics and music is witnessing the power specific performance cultures have on the selection, training, and evaluation of its participants. There is no doubt certain sport and music cultures attract, reward and develop perfectionistic self-talk in their performers. For example, golf and piano are very similar performance cultures. Both place a premium on correctness, require long hours of blocked practice (repetitions of the same movement pattern), and involve a great deal of solo practice. Both performance cultures consist primarily of individualized instruction emphasizing precise execution of highly technical movement patterns and the elimination of mistakes. As a result, coaches, instructors, and players in both performance cultures recognize the advantage of a perfectionistic mindset during practice repetitions. This does not suggest perfectionistic mindsets do not exist in other performance cultures because they do. However, some cultures, due to the nature of the tasks required, allow more leeway during performance. For example, a tennis player can play a poor point and still win a game, or play a bad game and win a set, or lose a set and still win a match. In golf or piano when you miss a shot or hit the wrong note, you can never get it back. You do not get a second chance to do it over. Therefore, perfection is a goal many golfers and pianists strive to attain. On the other end of the perfectionistic continuum might be basketball and jazz. Both require practicing set plays with agreed upon rules but allow for a great deal of creative adjustments or improvisation during performance.

Perfectionistic self-talk is grounded primarily in the Parent ego state. Persisting through difficulties, monitoring and judging execution, self-instructing technical correctness, and analyzing the causes and affects of mistakes, are all characteristic of the Critical Parent. An active Critical Parent is desirable when developing and refining the complex, precise and repeatable movement patterns necessary to improve technical skills. Therefore, having an overactive Critical Parent is rewarded both by instructors and developmental outcomes. However, your best performance outcomes occur when you are not judging, analyzing, or instructing.

Much like movement patterns that become automated through repetitive practice, critical self-talk patterns also become automated over time and through practice repetitions. Once these self-critical patterns become automated, they are initiated without conscious awareness. One way to break these critical patterns of the Adult ego state is to develop or expand your Natural Child.

EXPANDING YOUR NATURAL CHILD

It might be difficult to accurately recall what you were like as a young child while at play. Those times when there were no adults around and you were just playing, free from any analysis, judgements or self-critical thoughts. I remember, as a child, loving to build plastic models. I would spend hours fully engaged in the tedious construction of airplanes, tanks and cars. It is interesting for me to reflect upon the evolution of my model building skills as they coincided with the development of my Critical Parent. Initially, the models I built were crude with some misplaced parts, excess glue, and bad paint jobs but I was so proud of how they looked. As I became more skilled and my expectations for the finished product increased, I became more judgmental, self-critical, and concerned about getting things just right. Although this mindset helped me build better models, it often took away from the joy and natural connection I experienced during the building process. Over time, my reasons for building models changed from enjoying the process to producing a product that would meet the expectations of myself and others.

You may have experienced a similar evolution of your Critical Parent during your development as a musician. Although becoming more self-critical and judgmental of the finished product is necessary to develop and refine your skills as a musician; over time, these patterns of self-statements can wear down your confidence and diminish your ability to naturally connect with your music. To become a more confident performer you will need to reconnect with your Natural Child and replace the negative, critical self-statements with more positive thoughts, emotions and images. The following are three strategies for expanding your Natural Child and rediscovering the joy and passion of being a confident musician.

Be a Positive Self-coach

Self-coaching is a purposeful and directed inner dialogue that is much more than just positive thinking. Positive self-coaching is the ability to give yourself what you need mentally in order to stay positive, focused, and energized. Just like a good coach, there may be times when you need to talk to yourself in a harsh tone to regain focus, overcome fear, or correct a lackadaisical effort. However, more often than not, being a good self-coach involves *positive* self-coaching. To sustain a high level of effort, persist through difficulties, and maintain confidence, you must develop and refine your ability to coach yourself in positive ways.

Although, you can be a terrible self-coach and continue to practice with intensity and determination, you will never truly enjoy performing at a high level without being a positive self-coach. If you want to experience the childlike passion, fearless confidence, and relaxed focus, of a child at play, developing your ability to coach yourself in positive ways is a necessity.

Your inner dialogue is an important tool you can use to excel in practices, performances and in life. Think about the ways you talk to yourself when you are frustrated. What do you say to yourself to get optimistic and back on task? Chances are, you know what to say and how to say it. You probably could "coach" someone else in ways that keep them positive and focused, but how often do you apply this type of coaching to yourself? You know how to be a positive coach, you just do not apply it to yourself positively on a regular basis. Positive self-coaching involves talking to yourself in an affirmative way to stay focused and energized on the job at hand. The following are positive self-coaching statements I have found effective in helping musicians approach and respond to situations with greater confidence.

"What I already have is good enough, I don't need to do anything special": This is a useful self-coaching statement to repeat to yourself leading up to a performance. It is not unusual for musicians to feel they have not quite prepared enough or need to do something special during their performance to succeed. Sometimes these feelings result in a mild panic before a performance, resulting in excessive worry and self-defeating thoughts. The purpose of this coaching statement is to provide the belief to simply go with what you already have and that will be good enough. You will find, in most of your performances, you really do not need to do anything special to be successful. Thinking you need to do something special resulting in more problems than solutions.

"Accept and Adjust": You will find this self-coaching statement to be helpful in many areas of your life, not just music performance. The next time you find yourself frustrated due to an unexpected event, repeat to yourself the statement, "Accept and adjust." To accept means not judging the situation as good or bad but rather seeing it for what it is. Then, you can either adjust your attitude, allowing you to deal with the current situation better, or adjust your behavior so that you can respond more effectively. Acceptance of your current situation is a critical first step in developing alternative strategies for success. Think about how often you waste time and energy wishing things were different, feeling like you have been treated unfairly, or being frustrated by events you cannot control. Using this coaching statement will help you become more focused, confident, and solution oriented.

Stop, Clear and Replace: When you notice you are distracted by negative self-coaching, say to yourself "Stop," then clear your mind of negative thought(s), and replace them with a positive concentrative thought. As you absorb yourself in the new thought, the negative thinking will fade away. There are times before an important performance when a vivid image of a negative experience (past or future) may pop into your head. When this happens, stop the image or thought as soon as you notice it, clear your mind, and create a new positive image or thought to replace the negative one.

Express Positive Emotion

In many highly technical performance cultures such as piano and golf, it is much more acceptable to express negative emotion than it is to express positive emotion. The show of frustration following mistakes or poor performances is believed to be a sign that the student is trying hard. The expression of positive emotion following a great shot, or the flawless execution of a difficult passage, is not often accepted and is believed to lead to a more lackadaisical effort. Thinking back upon this past week, how often did you express negative emotions during your practice sessions compared to positive emotions?

I am not suggesting you should not express negative emotion, only that there should be a better balance with the expression of positive emotion if you want to expand your Natural Child. If you are like most musicians, you probably have a more difficult time expressing positive emotion and may struggle with understanding its true value. What do you think would happen if you made a commitment next week to express more positive emotion during your practice sessions?

Positive emotional self-coaching is allowing yourself to experience the pride of doing something well and joyful aspects of practicing your craft. One of the best things you can do for yourself during practice is giving yourself a high-five when you do something well. This can come as a fist pump, big smile, or raising your hands above your head. Either way, the goal is to genuinely feel good about what you just did. This is not intended to show up anyone, but to feel and express your joy. Many musicians have been socialized into believing that positive emotion is a sign of "cockiness" and expressing positive emotion is a sure way to lose friends. Think about how often you physically express a negative emotion compared to how often you express, and experience, a positive emotion. Which one is going to help you stay more confident, focused and trusting?

Use Positive Images

Another tool you can use to enhance your confidence and expand your Natural Child is the use of positive images. Just as you have random thoughts that enter your consciousness, you have random images. The effective use of positive images lies in your ability to consciously direct your images in a way that enhances your confidence.

When you imagine doing something well or doing something poorly, you are essentially talking to your motor memory system in a language to which it responds. Your motor memory system understands images much more clearly and vividly than it understands words. You will often see athletes visualizing specific movement patterns before executing (e.g., golf swing), trying to recall a particular kinetic "feel" from memory, or a musician visualizing the sound of an opening melody immediately before beginning a performance. Once the desired feel or rhythm is "locked in," musicians find it easier to trust their movements without consciously thinking about correctness.

Take a moment and try a brief imagery session. Start by closing your eyes and getting yourself comfortable and relaxed. You might want to focus your attention on your breathing with an emphasis on relaxing the muscles around your face and shoulders with each exhalation. Imagine yourself in your kitchen. You open your refrigerator and take out a juicy yellow lemon. You place it on the table and notice the texture of the skin and the beads of moisture. As you cut through it with a knife the lemon juice squirts out. You cut the lemon in quarters. As you bring it up to your mouth, you notice the lemon smell and the juice running down your fingers. Now bite into the lemon and feel the juice rush into your month. Chances are, if your image was vivid, you experienced a slight recoil from the lemon and a tightening sensation in the back of your jaw. This is a learned reflex for most people when biting into a lemon. The lesson learned is your mind does not always distinguish between a vivid image and reality.

Using positive images and stopping negative ones takes commitment and self-discipline. If you really want to become a more confident and trusting performer, use positive images on a regular basis. Mastery imagery involves visualizing yourself executing a skill or performing flawlessly under the conditions in which you will be performing. Developing a performance script and then reviewing it multiple times is a great place to start to get you thinking about and visualizing playing great.

PERFORMANCE CONFIDENCE

Coaches regularly ask their athletes before games or matches, "Are you ready?" This question is meant to get at the heart of pre-performance confidence. Meaning, are you mentally, physically and emotionally ready to fully extend yourself in this competition. Think of the last time you felt ready before a performance. What did being ready feel like to you? Where did your feeling of readiness and confidence come from? Perhaps you had a series of very good practices leading up to your performance. Maybe you were familiar with the piece you were going to play or had many positive experiences in the venue where you were about to perform. Whatever the case, your sense of readiness not only came from your ability to harness your mental and physical capabilities, but also your emotional capabilities. When performing music, focusing from beginning to end, remaining steady through the ups and downs, effectively handling the unexpected, and managing mistakes, are just as much an emotional test as they are a mental or physical test.

It can be helpful to imagine the process of instilling performance confidence as a funnel that is wide at the top then gradually narrows at the bottom. What happens from the top to the bottom of the funnel is a process of organizing your thoughts and emotions to create a confident performance mindset. The top of the funnel represents the general thoughts and practice activities that help you to refine your performance piece. This may take place one week to ten days before your performance. As you get closer to the performance date, your preparation becomes more mental, emotional and musical with the bottom of the funnel representing a confident mindset and heightened sense of readiness. Developing and engaging an effective pre-performance routine that acts like a funnel will facilitate your ability to transition from a practice mindset to a confident performance mindset necessary for playing your best when it counts.

Pre-Performance Practice

Your practice sessions during the week leading up to your performance should consist primarily of variable practice, developing and reviewing your performance script, and keeping your mental journal. Remember, variable practice is a performance practice format used to develop a more trusting mindset. For some musicians, variable practice before a performance is counter intuitive or inconsistent with their pervious experiences. They have relied almost exclusively on blocked practice leading up to a performance to build confidence in their ability to execute the movement patterns flawlessly. As was previously discussed, blocked practice often reinforces self-instruction, monitoring of correctness, and overanalysis of mistakes, increasing cognitive activity and a desire to control correctness. Variable practice, on the other hand, is used to build your concentration muscle and enhance your ability to trust and let go of conscious control. In essence, training your ability to trust during performance what you have trained in practice.

Another way to create a confident performance mindset is to put yourself under pressure during practices. Leaning into pressure means you regularly seek creative ways to test your mental performance skills during practice. Leaning away from pressure means you keep yourself in a skill development mode and do not challenge your comfort level. Pressure builds diamonds. Learn to lean into pressure instead of away from it. Musicians who regularly seek to create challenges and repeatedly find ways to put themselves under pressure in practice leading up to a performance get the quality performance repetitions necessary to develop a confident performance mindset.

Anticipating and preparing for difficult or distracting performance situations by simulating them in a practice environment is a strategy used by many musicians and athletes. One of the most familiar is playing loud crowd noise over the sound system during football practice to simulate the playing environment. This provides players with valuable game-like repetitions. For musicians, similar strategies are used when rehearsing with the television or radio playing in the background. The idea is to inoculate the musician to any auditory distractions that might occur during performance.

You can also create meaningful repetitions of effectively managing distracting situations by writing down possible distractors and developing responses in advance. This is a coping response exercise that can be turned into a coping imagery script. A coping imagery script involves creating a script of yourself responding effectively to various distractors (delayed performance start, excessive noise, poor acoustics, etc.) and, in your minds eye, visualizing yourself responding to the situations with confidence and poise. The goal of coping imagery is to anticipate possible distractions that may, or may not occur, and seeing yourself respond effectively. This form of imagery provides you with repetitions of dealing with specific distractions so, when or if they occur, you have practiced an effective response.

Additionally, making a performance script for a specific performance and rereading it a number of times leading up to your performance is a great way to build pre-performance confidence. Ideally, your script should be completed at least three days before your performance. This period provides you the opportunity to reread your script multiple times to create positive thoughts, feelings, and sensations of playing great. Similarly, keeping your High-performance Journal acts to build confidence and belief in your preparation by recording the best aspects of your practice sessions and other positive thoughts you have leading up to your performance.

Pre-Performance Routine

Your pre-performance routine should begin the day before your performance and end in the greenroom before walking out on stage. The goal of a pre-performance routine is to engage your spirit and passion to perform. Great athletes throughout history have understood the importance of pre-performance routines in getting themselves ready for battle and engaging their fighting spirit. As a musician, your fighting spirit will take on a different form. You are fighting to win the inner battle. To have the courage to trust what you already have, to let go of conscious control, and to fully express the feelings and emotions in your music. This is a courageous act requiring you to marshal your mental and emotional resources to get it done.

Keep in mind what you need emotionally to prepare yourself may not be what others need to prepare themselves. It is possible those closest to you, including friends, family, and even your instructor, may not fully understand what you need to get yourself emotionally prepared to perform. Maybe your best friend is someone who needs complete silence and solitude to prepare for her performance. You might have an ensemble member who needs to talk excessively to stay loose or an instructor who needs to talk you through your "game plan" a few times before he feels you are ready to perform. People prepare differently. Therefore, it is not only important to understand how you best prepare for a performance, but also to anticipate differences in preparation needed by others and not get thrown off or distracted by them.

A pre-performance routine involves a sequence of activities designed to prepare your mind, body, and emotions for your immediate performance. It is important you are able to transition and prepare for the demands of the performance situation you are about to face and get started on the right foot. If you find that you are a slow starter or it is sometimes difficult for you to "get your head ready to perform," then a solid pre-performance routine is that much more important.

Although having a solid preparation routine is common among the best performers, they understand adjustments are sometimes necessary due to unforeseen events (weather, change in start times, etc.). When you are unable to complete your entire preparation routine, there is no need to panic. Effective adjustments can be made, especially when planned in advance.

Game Plan: The goal of developing a pre-performance game plan is to give you a global picture of what your "game day" will look like so you know where you need to be and when you need to be there. The use of a pre-performance game plan is one of the most effective strategies you can use to control your performance anxiety and create a feeling of readiness. A pre-performance game plan is a thought out series of events that provide a structure to the time you spend leading up to your performance. It provides a structured pattern of activities that enhance your ability to approach difficult and demanding performances with a greater sense of control. A solid game plan will help you shift gears into the mental and emotional mindset needed to perform your best. Although, your game plan involves a pre-planned structure, your planned activities are not "fixed" and may be adjusted throughout the day leading up to your performance.

Walk Through: Your pre-performance walk through takes place the day or night before your performance and is different from a rehearsal. A pre-performance walk though is designed to emotionally attune you with the physical environment in which you will be performing. It could last from five to fifteen minutes and may involve walking around the stage and venue or sitting in your performance environment imagining yourself playing relaxed, confidence and focused. Your performance environment is usually more electric and sometimes more chaotic than a practice environment and attuning to this reality gives you a greater sense of preparation leading up to your performance.

Warm-up: When you arrive onsite before your performance, what do you do to create the feeling you are ready to perform? Do you have a structured warm-up that you have practiced and can move through in a predetermined amount of time? Being emotionally and mentally prepared to perform your best requires you to not only develop a structured warm-up routine, but to practice this routine. Although your physical warm-up goals for a performance may be similar to a practice session, your mental goals should be different from a typically practice warm-up, specifically, clearing your mind of distractions and visualizing playing great in your performance environment. You will find when you are able to accomplish these mental goals during your pre-performance warm-up, it becomes much easier to accomplish them during performance. I suggest that you have two structured pre-performance warm-up routines, a Plan A, and Plan B. Plan A, is your ideal warm-up. You have no time restrictions and complete control over your warm-up activities. Plan B, is an abbreviated pre-performance warm-up (e.g., 20 minutes), and includes only the essential warm-up activities needed to get you mentally, physically and emotionally ready to perform.

Greenroom Ritual: The goal of your greenroom ritual is to emotionally connect with the inner battle, to harness your courage, and trust your training during performance. A greenroom ritual, like a locker room ritual for athletes, can take many different forms depending on the individual performer and the specific performance demands. For example, some performers sit quietly in a chair and mentally rehearse parts of their event. Others like to walk around and take their mind off performing until a few minutes before going out on stage. Find what works for you and stick with it. Musicians who effectively connect with the emotional aspects of performing in their greenroom ritual tend to start better and finish stronger.

PERFORMANCE EVALUATION

Although, commitment to being prepared is a key to confidence, how you evaluate performances is critical for sustaining your confidence throughout a performance season. Most musicians have not experienced the power of a solid *post*-performance routine. Typically, upon completion of a performance, musicians will meet with family, friends, and their instructor who may comment on various positive and negative aspects of the performance. It is important for you to make some personal time to reflect upon the effectiveness of your pre-performance routine and the mental and emotional aspects of your performance. This post-performance evaluation is an important part of developing and refining your mental performance skills and your performance preparation.

Many musicians have found it helpful to keep a post-performance journal where they spend roughly twenty minutes reflecting upon and writing down specific, positive mental and emotional aspects regarding their performance and their preparation routines. This is time well spent! Keeping a post-performance journal is perhaps the best tool you can use to instill and maintain your confidence.

POSTSCRIPT

If you had to choose one psychological attribute that, if you developed to its fullest, would make the greatest positive contribution to your performance as a musician which one would it be? Over the past several years, I have asked this question to performers from a variety of domains. The most common responses are psychological attributes related to self-belief or self-confidence. Many musicians understand the power that believing in themselves, their abilities, and their preparation has on their performance outcomes. When musicians are confident in themselves and what they are doing; they focus better, are more relaxed under pressure; and are more decisive and trusting during performance.

Are you doing everything you can to become a more confident musician? Although practicing long hours is important to developing belief in yourself, it is not sufficient. Being physically, technically and musically prepared to perform is not the same as being mentally and emotionally prepared to perform. You probably have a number of strategies for training yourself to memorize and execute the physical and musical aspects of a performance. Do you also engage in activities that develop your mental and emotional preparedness?

SELF-REFLECTION QUESTIONS

1. Think about the impression you communicate to your audience during performances regarding your belief in yourself and your music when you answer the following questions. Develop a message or statement to put on your shirt which best describes the impression you *currently* give the audience during a performance. Describe how you give this impression. The behavior, body language, facial expressions, and attitudes communicate this message (e.g., I will find some way to screw this up; facial tension, low energy, timid walk).

My current Message:

2. Create a message to put on your shirt which best describes the impression you would *like to* give your audience. Describe how you would give this impression? The behaviors, body language, facial expressions, and attitudes that would best communicate this message (e.g., I am prepared for this challenge; relaxed focus, confident walk, smiling)

Desired Message:

3. Describe specific strategies you can use to put yourself under pressure during practices. The practice activities can you implement to create the thoughts and emotions you typically experience during an important performance (e.g., perform entire recital without warm-up, video tape or playing with television on).

	Strategies for creating pressure
1	
2	
3	

4. Develop two pre-performance routines, Plan A and Plan B. Write down specific activities, goals, foe each and estimated time for completion. The Plan A warm-up is used when you have an unlimited amount of time and the Plan B is an abbreviated warm-up (about 20-minutes) that you can use when necessary.

Plan A Warm-up

	Activity	Est. Time	Purpose or Goal
1			
2			
3			
4			
5			
6			

Total time needed: _____

Plan B Warm-up

	Activity	Est. Time	Purpose or Goal
1			
2			
3			
4			
5			
6			

Total time needed: _____

5
Managing Your Attentional Focus

The Lioness

A loud noise in the forest turned out to be a group of animals in a raucous debate about which of them could produce the largest litter.

A mouse bragged, "I had eight babies at once! Try to beat that."

"That's nothing," a muskrat snickered. "I had ten babies in my litter."

A fox saw a lioness sitting quietly nearby and sneered: "How many cubs did you have in your litter?"

"Only one this time," she proudly replied, "but it's a lion!"

In the fable of the Lioness, the debate over which animal produced the highest quality litter was brought into perspective when the lioness indicated, though she only had one baby: it was a lion. A similar debate over the value of quantity versus quality of practice can be heard in the halls of music schools. However, one thing is clear, if you want quality practices or a high level performances, you must focus your attention deliberately and effectively. You perform best when you are completely absorbed, fully engaged, and beautifully connected to what you are doing in the present moment.

Often as a musician, you play the role of performance psychologist trying to figure out the best way to practice, memorize material, prepare for an upcoming performance, or best handle a crushingly bad performance. Learning to effectively manage your attentional focus, like these other mental skills is typically learned through trial-and-error. Yet concentration is one of the most common mental skills linked to performance outcomes and, least understood.

You often hear teachers imploring students to "just concentrate," but what does this mean? Concentration is obviously important. Think how often you attribute a solid performance to good concentration and a poor performance to bad concentration. There is no debate that great musicians are able to focus their attention more effectively, deal with distractions better, and have fewer lapses in attention than other musicians. One of the reasons concentration is difficult to understand is, during your best performances, concentration feels like non-focus. Your performance unfolds naturally and automatically and you are totally connected to and absorbed with the task at hand.

This chapter discusses aspects of focusing and refocusing your attention, how anxiety and heightened physiology affects your ability to concentrate effectively, and provides tools to improve your ability to manage your attentional focus during both practices and performances.

CHARACTERISTICS OF CONCENTRATION

Concentration refers to the mental effort required to direct your attentional focus to process specific task related information. In other words, *optimal concentration is the ability to consciously focus attention on a specific task, for a particular time, and with a desired intensity.* How long you stay focused on the task at hand and the intensity of your focus will ultimately determine if you are concentrating or just briefly focusing your attention.

When you are concentrating effectively, you are focusing your full attention onto relevant information necessary for you to perform your best. During performance, your mind is both consciously and subconsciously processing information from both internal and external sources. For example, when sight reading during performance, much of the information processed takes place in your subconscious (e.g., rapid and precise finger movements), but you are also required to consciously direct your attentional focus on the musical score in order to process necessary information correctly. To understand how this processing takes place it is important to recognize the characteristics of concentration. These include; the direction, width, and selectivity of attentional focus.

Direction and Width of Focus

One of the most obvious aspects of concentration is the direction of your focus, or the object of your attention. It is helpful to view concentration as having both direction (Internal/External) and width (Broad/Narrow) of focus. You can focus your attention on something *internal* such as your thoughts, a specific sound you rehearse in your imagination, or a feeling in your fingers. You can also choose to focus on something *external* to yourself in the physical environment such as sights, sounds, or smells.

The width of your focus refers to the breadth of information to which you are attending. When your attention is focused in a *broad* fashion, you are attending to a variety of informational sources, either internally (e.g., your inner dialogue), or externally (e.g., listing to the sound of an orchestra). A *narrow* focus might be attending to one specific self-statement or listening to one specific instrument in the orchestra. Robert Niediffer added a great deal to the understanding of concentration by explaining that the width and direction of attention exist on two separate continuums, creating four attentional quadrants (see diagram). These are: External/Narrow (EN), External/Broad (EB), Internal/Narrow (IN) and Internal/Broad (IB).

To better understand the types of information processed in each attentional quadrant, consider the sequence of attentional shifts during a typical golf shot. Starting in Quadrant 1, the golfer will visually *assess* the situation by attending to the layout of the hole. "I am in the fairway 150 yards from the green with bunkers on the left and right." After attending to these external factors, the golfer will then *analyze* these factors and develop a game plan for this shot. "This shot requires a full-swing 7-iron." Once the shot is determined, the golfer will then *rehearse* the swing, feeling the swing tempo or recalling a swing thought. Finally, the golfer will *focus* on the target, then on the ball, before initiating the swing. These shifts in attention provide a structured focus that allows the golfer to process the necessary information needed to select and execute the best golf swing for this particular shot. When this sequence of attentional shifts is practiced correctly it builds the golfer's concentration capacity allowing for greater focus and correct information processing. When done consistently before each shot, this sequence of attentional shifts makes up the pre-shot concentration routine.

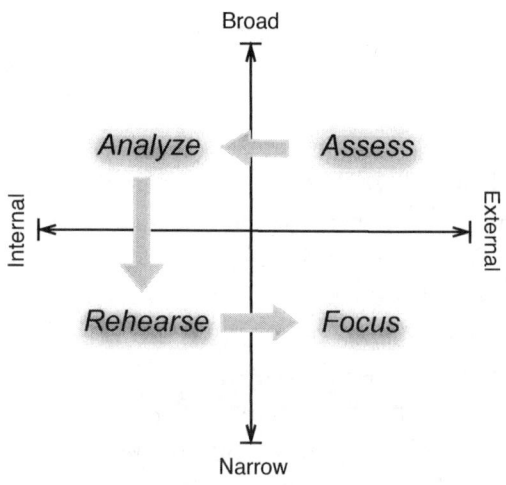

On the other hand, a bassoonist may start in the first quadrant (Broad/External), assessing the elements of the written score, then move to the second quadrant (Broad/Internal) listening to the opening melody in her mind. In quadrant three (Internal/Narrow), she listens to specific notes or plays the first phrases in her head. It is important to stay focused for a moment in quadrant three but not to perform only in that focus area. In quadrant four (External/Narrow), she focuses on the task at hand – the sound of the performance. This should be a place where the she relies on what was rehearsed in the previous three quadrants and trusts her ability to execute the performance with ease and relaxed focus and concentration.

Selectivity of Focus

One important aspect of music performance is the ability to select the correct attentional cues from the many irrelevant and competing cues. For the chamber musician to be able to read music, listen to ensemble members, determine and adjust sound, or count while playing an instrument is an extraordinary feat in attention-selecting and just one example of the complexity of focusing, refocusing and shifting attention during performance.

Attentional Shift: Virtually all performances require the musician to shift attentional focus to various selected and meaningful aspects throughout the duration of a performance. Shifting your focus from listening to the sound, feeling the emotion in the music, finding your place on the written score, are just a few examples of attentional shifts that are often required for a successful performance.

To be a great musician, you must not only be able to shift your attentional focus, but shift your focus at the optimal time. Many concentration errors occur when you shift too slowly or too rapidly from one focus point to another. One example of shifting too slowly might be a wind ensemble player who, analyzing the feeling of her reed, fails to enter in at the correct time. You can also shift your attention temporally, meaning you can focus on performance aspects that have occurred in the *past* (a missed note), are occurring in the *present* (the sound of your

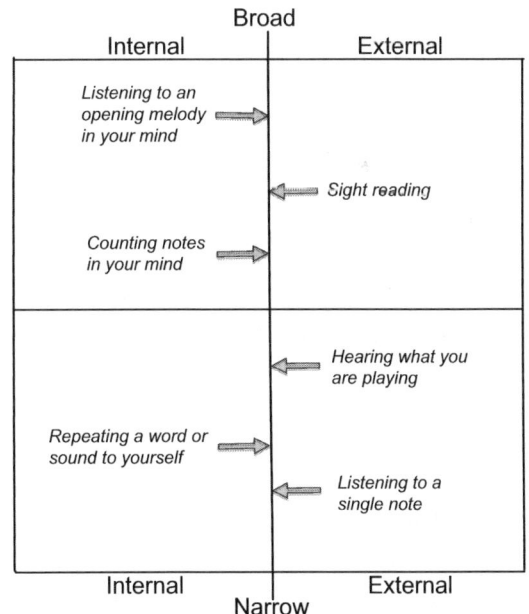

instrument), or will occur in the *future* (an upcoming difficult section). Most mature musicians understand the negative performance consequences of shifting and then holding their attention on past mistakes or distractions and have learned to quickly refocus back to the present moment or task at hand. However, similar negative consequences can occur when shifting and holding your focus on future aspects of performance. It is the holding of attentional focus that separates an attentional shift from an attentional scan.

Attentional Scan: Scanning of your attentional focus describes those moments when you consciously or subconsciously shift your attention while very briefly holding your focus point. An example of an attentional scan is when you quickly check your side view, then rear view mirrors while driving your car. You will continue scanning until something unusual or unexpected "captures" your attention, resulting in an attentional shift. Attentional scanning is done quickly and with little attentional effort. Consider a soccer player who mentally scans the positions of the defensive players while dribbling the ball up the field, seeing a teammate break into a seam, quickly scans the defensive backs position, makes the decision to kick the ball, then looks at the ball and kicks it. All within five-seconds. Although, these shifts in attention happen quickly and often below conscious awareness, each one is necessary for correct information processing and a successful pass.

Like the soccer player, your performances require you to make appropriate attentional shifts, and scan performance aspects quickly and effortlessly when necessary (e.g., body posture, muscle tension, hand placement, tempo, etc.). Being able to scan and shift attentional focus easily and effectively is a fundamental component of attentional flexibility. There are also shifts in attentional focus that happen unintentionally. These are called attentional drifts.

Attentional Drifts: Unlike attentional shifting and scanning, attentional drifts are unintentional and often begin below conscious awareness. During a performance your attention may drifting off to some irrelevant thought or image, only to realize it just in time to refocus back to your performance. For some musicians, attentional drifts occur quite frequently, especially during less demanding sections of s performance.

Your attentional focus is constantly in a state of flux, shifting, scanning, or drifting every minute of the day. In fact, it is more accurate to define effective concentration as your ability to refocus your attention back to the task-at-hand, rather than defining concentration as your ability to focus your attention on a specific task.

REFOCUSING YOUR ATTENTION

The nature of our world today requires us to skillfully manage our attention if we are to be both productive and happy. What we choose to focus on, and choose to ignore, greatly affect what we do and how we feel about what we do. For example, multitasking (quickly and effectively shifting and refocusing attention) has become a necessity and even a badge of honor for many individuals as they meet the many competing demands in their day. However, multitasking as an overdeveloped attentional skill, inhibits your ability to sustain the type of focus often needed for significant relationships and other high quality experiences. Multitasking is not good or bad, it just works against the type of sustained focus needed to be fully engaged.

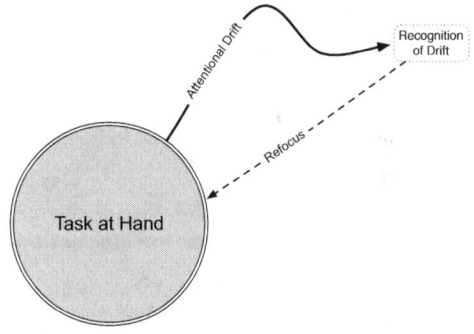

Holding your attention on a single object, thought, sound, feeling or even in the present moment, is a performance skill. High quality concentration needed to perform your best includes both shifting your focus effectively and holding your focus, allowing you to process the necessary information needed to meet your performance demands. Almost all human performances require focusing and refocusing repetitions throughout the performance duration. How much time you spend focused on the task-at-hand is greatly dependent upon your ability to recognize when you are off-task and refocus back to the task. I am sure you have had the experience of reading a few pages in a book, stopping and looking up and wondering to yourself what you just read. You had spent the last few minutes completely disengaged from the meaning of the words on the pages you read and were focused on something completely unrelated to the written material. In this case, minutes may have passed before you recognized your attentional drift and then refocused.

Concentration Muscle

Think of concentration as a muscle. Imagine each time you refocus back to the task-at-hand as one repetition of curling a weight with your biceps muscle. Each time you lose focus you are extending the weight away from your body. When you curl the weight again, or refocus back to the task, you have completed another repetition. It is the focus-refocus repetitions that build your concentration muscle. These repetitions build your concentration muscle which then allow you to focus more intensely and for longer periods of time, much like training a muscle allows you to generate greater force for longer periods of time. The more repetitions you can complete in a single session, the longer you focus on the task at hand and the bigger your concentration muscle will become. In other words, learning to discern when you are distracted and having the presence of mind to refocus, is at the heart of concentration during performance. It is this focus-refocus repetition that builds task concentration, much like the contraction-relaxation-contraction repetition that builds stronger, less fatigued muscles.

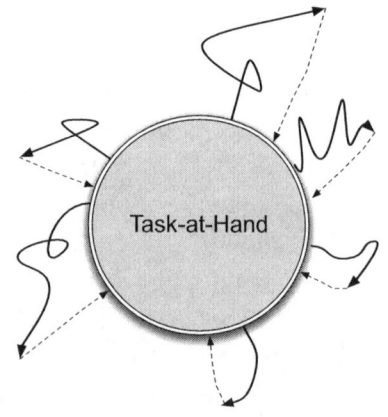

CONCENTRATION AND ANXIETY

Anxiety can be viewed as an interaction between your physiological and your attentional processes. Anxiety is often experienced as a nervous feeling with an accompanying sense of fear or apprehension. As your anxiety increases, your ability to effectively manage your attentional focus decreases. Although, some feeling of nervousness may facilitate your focus, once it reaches a level resulting in anxious thoughts and fears, you will loose your ability to process information accurately and effortlessly. This decrement in information processing, or cue utilization, can be explained by a loss of attentional flexibility and perceptual narrowing that occur as a result of heightened anxiety.

Loss of Attentional Flexibility

Flexibility of attentional focus describes your ability to move around the attentional quadrants effectively and efficiently when shifting or scanning. As previously mentioned, your ability to processes the correct information at the appropriate time is necessary to perform successfully. Holding your focus too long on one aspect of performance (e.g., a past mistake) or shifting to an irrelevant performance aspect (e.g., what others are thinking) can result in a memory laps or may cause you miss important informational cues (e.g., your place in the written music).

Your anxiety level often dictates the degree of attentional flexibility. Performance tasks that require large amounts of information processing, or a high degree of fine motor control cannot tolerate high levels of physiological arousal associated with anxiety. For example, a race car driver traveling at speeds over 200 miles per hour must process information from a variety of sources quickly and effortlessly. Not only must the driver visually attend to and anticipate what is happening in front of his car, he must also listen to his spotter and crew chef, while also feeling the cars handling capabilities. To accomplish this feat he must keep his physiology under control despite the severe consequences of making a mistake at high speeds.

Perceptual Narrowing

Increases in anxiety not only affect your ability to shift your attention appropriately, but heightened anxiety also narrows your focus, eliminating task-relevant cues. To better understand the relationship between anxiety and perceptual narrowing, think of your width of focus as a beam of light. When you are bored or lackadaisical, the beam is too broad (Focus A) and you are attending to many different information cues; both relevant to your performance (e.g., the sound you are producing) and irrelevant to your performance (e.g., audience noises). In this example, you would be under-aroused physiologically and your performance would not likely be optimal. If you realized your poor focus and coached yourself to "get your head back into the game," your physiology increases and your beam of light narrows so that you are now focusing totally on the task at hand with no other irrelevant stimuli (focus B) resulting in a more optimal performance. If, on the other hand, after making a mistake, you start to panic and your physiology increases, the beam of light narrows to a point where you miss some important performance cues, causing you to make another error (focus C). Being overanxious results in both a narrowing of your attention and an inability to shift your attention appropriately when necessary. Therefore, keeping your physiology under control is critical to managing your attentional focus before and during performance.

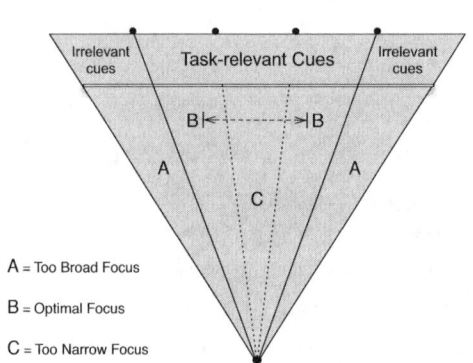

CONCENTRATION STRATEGIES

Concentration strategies can be used to either get you focused for the next task or to refocus back to the task at hand once you have been distracted. Read through the concentration strategies below and think of examples of how you can use each during a practice or performance.

Refocus Thoughts

Knowing you are thinking distracting thoughts and refocusing back to the task at hand is essential to good concentration. The goal of refocusing is to create the proper mindset for the upcoming task by clearing your mind of thoughts or other distractions from a previous task or event, and reestablishing the proper focus for the new task. Below are three simple ways for you to refocus after negative or distracting thoughts and emotions.

Breathe and Focus: One way to get your focus back to the task at hand either following a mistake or following a pause in your performance, is to breathe and focus. Here you take a deep breath clearing all thoughts and muscle tension as you exhale and then focus all your attention onto the immediate task at hand. For example, when feeling frustrated with your inability to make a technical correction during practice, you can stop, take a deep breath (clearing your mind and relaxing you muscles) then refocus back to the immediate task. This can also be used during performance as you transition from an "off" period to and "on" period during an orchestral performance.

Park-it: When you are experiencing high negative emotion in response to a mistake, you may find it helpful to remind yourself to "park" the negative emotion for the time being so you can complete your task. You do not need to try to abandon or eliminate the emotion altogether, simply put it on hold and come back to it later after your performance. For example, you may have had an emotional argument before a performance. There is nothing you can do to correct the situation at this time so "park" your emotion, refocus on the task at hand and deal with the situation later.

Act As If: When you are fearful or have self-doubts going into a performance, you can remind yourself to "act as if" you are a confident and prepared performer. Body language has a very powerful effect on your attitude and your immediate focus. Acting 'as if" is one way to adjust your body language (e.g., posture, facial expression, and gate) which often produces confident, positive thoughts. You may have the experience of walking into a room full of strangers and someone says to you, "act as if you own the place." Looking and acting confident and positive will help you control negative, self-defeating thoughts and allow you to focus on what you need to be doing to play your best. This can also be very helpful when walking on stage for a performance.

Refocus Plans

A refocus plan involves anticipating possible distractions that might occur before and during a particular performance and developing refocusing strategies for each distraction. In essence, you have developed a pre-planned response for a particular distraction so, when it happens, you are prepared and can quickly and effectively manage it and move on. Writing down your responses will also give you the opportunity to visualize yourself effectively managing these distractions. This is similar to the process of going into a job interview having anticipated certain questions and prepared your answers in advance. Certainly, the interviewer will not ask all the questions you anticipated, but you are much better prepared to answer the ones that are asked. Although there will be unexpected distractions, many of the potential distractions for an upcoming performance can be anticipated based on previous performance experiences or knowledge of the upcoming performance demands. Below is an example of a refocus plan for three anticipated distractions.

Distraction	Refocusing Response
1. Stressed-out instructor before performance	Keep conversation short and make time to be alone
2. Poor warm-up leading into performance	Remind myself I've had poor warm-ups before a played great

Focus Plans

Focus plans are like a map of your attentional focus during performance. Developing a focus plan is a technique used in a variety of performance domains to help performers identify how best to focus, and refocus, during their performance. Focus plans provide you with an "at-a-glance" visual understanding of the concentration demands of your performance piece and allow you the opportunity to pre-plan and practice desirable attentional shifts. Your focus plan should provide a very general structure of a piece, outlining significant factors that change the mood or character during a performance (e.g., drastic key changes, sudden tempo shifts, long dramatic pauses, abrupt dynamic changes). By mapping out these elements, you develop a broader sense of direction that applies to the entire piece. Focus plans will also help to maintain your focus during the entire performance by creating smaller goals and pre-planned moments of releasing and then regaining focus built into the interpretation of the piece.

Focus plans are very individual and can take many forms. The following are two examples you may draw upon when developing your own focus plan. The first is an example of a tennis focus plan and the second, a plan developed by a pianist. Draw upon the differences in these two plans to create a focus plan that best suits your needs.

Tennis Focus Plan: The sport of tennis, like many performances in music, has both on-periods and off-periods. In tennis, these periods can be divided into "during the point" - when you are on, or playing, and "between the point" - when you are off or not playing. A single tennis game consists of many "on" and "off" periods. How well you manage your attention between points or during the off periods is often an indicator of how well you will focus during the point.

Below is a focus plan for a tennis point that provides a broader understanding of how you might map your attentional focus for your own music performances. As you will notice, the between point attentional shifts are divided into three phases: Respond, Refocus, and Ready. The goal during the point is to Trust or Release. The purpose of structuring between point shifts is to increase the player's ability to trust and release conscious control during the point.

This plan indicates, once the point has ended, the player will respond, refocus onto the game plan for the upcoming point, and mentally prepare (ready) immediately before the point begins. To fully trust and release conscious control requires mental readiness. Although, this readiness can be brief, it is still a necessary and perhaps the most important part of the between point phase. During the Ready phase, the mental goal is to gather attentional focus into the present and clear your mind. This can be accomplished through a simple "breathe and focus" process where you take a deep breath,

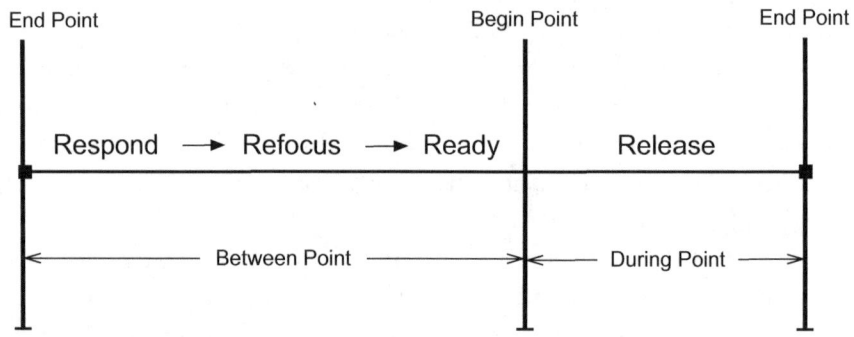

relaxing your muscles and clearing your mind as you exhale, then bring your focus to the present task at hand. During the point, the goal is to keep a trust focus (clear and present) and releasing conscious control over correctness.

Piano Focus Plan: Below is an example of a Liebesträume (Franz Liszt) focus plan created by a pianist. As you can see, you can be creative in developing your own map key that relates the symbols used in the focus plan with a brief explanation for each symbol. You can choose to be as detailed as you like depending on what provides the most meaning without being distracting. Once you have finished your focus plan, visualize yourself playing your piece while following your plan.

Managing Your Attentional Focus 117

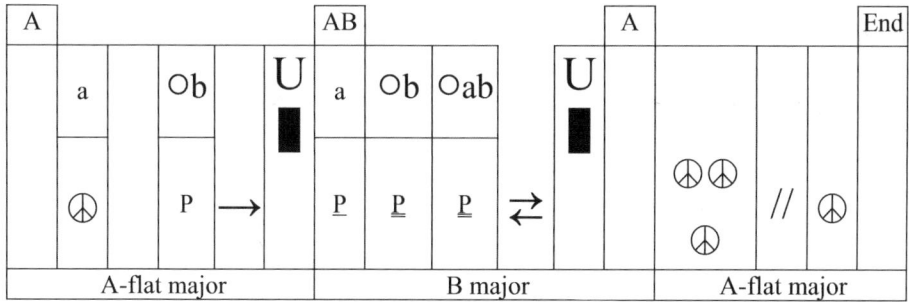

Map key for *Liebesträume* focus plan

☮ = Peaceful character initiated with relaxed breaths and a more delicate touch or tone
P = Passionate character
P̲ = Increase in Passion
P̲ = Continued Increase in Passion (more agitated)
→ = Keep the intensity going to the end of the section.
⇄ = Maintain a circular focus to keep the intensity
U = Pause. Keep sonorities ringing from previous section while mentally preparing for next section.
// = Slight break in sound, peaceful sonority is prepared.
▆ = Complete stop. Focus should begin fresh at the start of the next section.
○ = Refocus concentration

The goal of a focus plan is to provide you with specific *attentional targets* to hit throughout your performance. The primary benefit of preplanning these targets and practicing them is to provide mental anchors that keep you focused on trusting the musicality of your playing. This is especially helpful during performances in which you are anxious. Although different types of performance domains (e.g., music, sport and dance) have unique task demands affecting the optimal focus needed for best performances, each can benefit from developing a focus plan. Focus plans are specifically designed to use as a practice strategy to build your concentration muscle and help you focus better during performance.

POSTSCRIPT

What you choose to pay attention to or ignore greatly affects the quality of your experiences and performances. The skillful management of your attention is the key to improving virtually every aspect of your experience as a musician: from mood to musicality, to motivation for practice. What do you think would happen to your performances if you increased the quality of your concentration during practice by just 20 percent? Notice that I said *during practice*. Quality practice is all about quality focus and quality repetitions. Just as in the fable, you are much better off with one quality repetition than with eight repetitions of lesser quality.

SELF-REFLECTION QUESTIONS

1. Knowing where you want to go is half the battle to getting there. This is why it is important to know the optimal focus needed to meet the specific task demands in your performance. Using the concentration quadrants, identify four tasks necessary for your best performance and place them in their appropriate quadrants (e.g., reading the musical score (EB) or focusing on the breathing process (IB).

	Tasks	Quadrants
1		
2		
3		
4		

Managing Your Attentional Focus 119

2. Is there one quadrant that is best for you to be in during your performance? If so, which is it and why? If not, why not?

_____

_____

3. Which quadrant tends to dominate when you become overanxious? Explain.

_____

_____

_____

4. Using the explanations and examples in this chapter, develop a focus plan selecting a piece you have memorized so your focus plan can be created without any music in front of you to avoid making the plan too detailed. Begin by identifying the major sections of the work and symbolize them in any way that makes sense to you. Locate significant changes within the piece (key changes, tempo, dynamics, etc.). Create your own map key to relate the symbols used with a brief explanation for each symbol that makes sense within the context of the piece. Finally, visualize yourself playing the piece while following your focus plan and make any adjustments you deem necessary. Once you have a focus plan in place, practice your plan on a regular basis and see for yourself how it increases your ability to focus correctly and trust during your performance.

5. Provide examples of five distractions you might experience either before or during an upcoming performance. Think through specific refocusing responses for each. It is best to develop a similar list for yourself at least one week before your performance. Ideally, you do not want to be focused on possible distractions the day before or the day of a performance. Unlike a Performance Script, which is helpful to read and visualize the days leading up to a performance, your refocus plan is best developed and reviewed early in the week so you can focus your

energy on playing great (e.g., missed note; focus on plan and forget past)

	Distraction	Refocusing Response
1		
2		
3		
4		
5		

6
Creating A Positive Performance Mindset

You Never Know

Nasrudin sometimes took people for trips in his boat. One day a pedagogue hired him to ferry him across a very wide river. As soon as they were afloat, the scholar asked whether it was going to be rough.

"Don't ask me nothing about it," said Nasrudin.
"Have you never studied grammar?"
"No," said the mulla.
"In that case, half your life has been wasted."

The mulla said nothing. Soon a terrible storm blew up. The mulla's crazy cockleshell was filling with water. He leaned over toward his companion. "Have you ever learned to swim?"

"No," said the pedant.

"In that case, schoolmaster, <u>all</u> your life is lost for we are sinking."

If you are like most people, you probably studied many things in school you never thought would apply to the real world. You may have even believed that, "Half your life" has been wasted studying things that do not seem to matter. Even today you can walk the halls of almost any university and hear the popular refrain, "When am I ever going to use this stuff?" Of course, the process of learning such things is helping to teach you how to think and, hopefully, opening your mind to new ideas. Unlike the facts and formulas you cram into your mind for exams and quickly forget, learning how to create a positive performance mindset is a skill that will serve you well throughout the rest of your life.

The world's greatest coaches, managers, and teachers have often said, "Attitude is everything." What is an attitude and how does it affect your thoughts, emotions and behaviors? Your attitude is a mindset consisting of the thoughts and feelings preceding, and often dictating, your behaviors. It is your mindset that determines not only how you *approach* situations but also how you *respond* to situations in your life, your practices, and your performances. Your mindset is the mental energy and focus you *choose* to bring to situations. How you approach and respond is a choice you make. If that is true, then choosing your attitude, or your mindset is, to a large extent, the most powerful choice you make everyday!

How well you manage your thoughts and emotions is essential to playing your best when it counts. It is not the presence or absence of fears, self-doubts, feelings of nervousness, or anxiety that distinguish the best performers from the others. Most high level performers in sport, business, and performing arts, experience some level of all these thoughts and emotions before and sometimes during important events. The distinction between the best and the rest lies in the ability to manage these negative emotions, not in the ability to eliminate them all together. Although great musicians usually look comfortable when they are performing, you can bet their performances do not always start out feeling that way. Generally, performance is not about being comfortable, it is about being uncomfortable and effectively managing your discomfort. In other words, if you are striving to be comfortable before and during your performances, then you are striving for the wrong goal.

The goal of this chapter is to help you create a positive performance mindset for your performances and help you *want to have* a positive mindset more often. You must agree there are times when it feels better to be negative, frustrated, or angry than it does to be positive, composed, and focused. When feeling distressed, taken advantage of, or unappreciated, the last thing you may want to do is be positive. Knowing how to turn your attitude around is one thing, having the motivation or will to do so is quite another. Attitude IS everything, and effective performers have learned how to create the proper attitude and bring positive energy and focus to what they do, even when they do not feel like it.

PERFORMANCE ANXIETY

Believe or not, I taught eight semesters of a performance psychology class to graduate music students without saying the words, "performance anxiety." In my opinion, it represents one of the most overused and misunderstood terms among musicians. I have found it similar to the term "burnout" used by many young athletes. Both these ideas are used as catchall phrases that mean many different, and even "scary" things. For example, if your hands shake, if you think wild negative thoughts, or if you have memory slips during performances, you are told you are experiencing performance anxiety. This, in a round about way, makes it worse by implying you have a "psychological issue" that, if not addressed, may become debilitating.

Similarly, young athletes who say they do not want to practice their sport anymore, or want to take a few weeks off from competition, are said to be burn out. In both cases, what is often occurring has not been described accurately. For this reason, the terms performance anxiety and burnout should be used sparingly and accurately. The implications of these terms seem much more far reaching than they should be. From my experiences most musicians, like most athletes, will experience anxiety before, and often during, a performance and may become emotionally stale and physically exhausted at times during a long competitive season. I do not want to discount the percentage of people who do experience debilitating anxiety before a performance or who are clinically burn out. My concern is we do not make things worse for the majority of musicians who can benefit from mental skills training.

For the purposes of this chapter, anxiety will be defined as a heightened mental and physical response to the perceived threat inherent in most evaluative situations (i.e., performances). You will often feel anxiety as a type of fear, or apprehension, and experience the accompanying thoughts (e.g., worry, self-doubt) and physiology (e.g., increased heart rate, shallow breathing, muscle tremors, dry mouth). Any time you enter into an evaluative or competitive situation and *care about doing well*, you will experience some level of anxiety. When you perform, you are likely to perceive your performance as a type of evaluation (by yourself and by others), or possibility a competition with other musicians and, therefore, you will experience a heightened level of physiology before performing. It is the combination of perceived demands, consequences, and corresponding physiological responses, that is commonly referred to as performance anxiety.

PERFORMANCE EFFECTS OF ANXIETY

A positive performance mindset means you are keeping your anxiety within certain limits enabling you to be mentally alert and focused while being physically relaxed. If your physiology is too low (under-aroused) you may be physically relaxed but have difficultly focusing correctly (e.g., lackadaisical or bored). Conversely, if your physiology is too high, your performance will be adversely affected by excessive muscle tension and loss of focus control.

A commonly accepted explanation of the relationship between your physiological response and your performance level can be found in the theory of optimal arousal. This hypothesis suggests increases in your physiological arousal will produce commensurate performance improvement until it reaches an optimal level resulting in your best performance; after which, greater increases in your physiology will inhibit performance. This effect creates an inverted U picture (see diagram). The level of optimal physiological activation depends on the nature of the performance task. For example, highly computational tasks (e.g., chess, complex mathematics) or tasks that involve accuracy of fine motor control (e.g., piano, golf putting) require lower levels of physiological activation to perform optimally. While tasks involving larger muscle groups and explosive movements (e.g., football tackle, weight lifting) or lack complexity (e.g., yelling at the top of your lungs) are best achieved with high levels of physiological activation.

An important characteristic of your performance mindset is the management of your physiological and cognitive response allowing you to move your arousal up or down, depending on what is needed for you to be alert, confident, and focused. In other words, your ability to manage your anxiety level, not just reduce it.

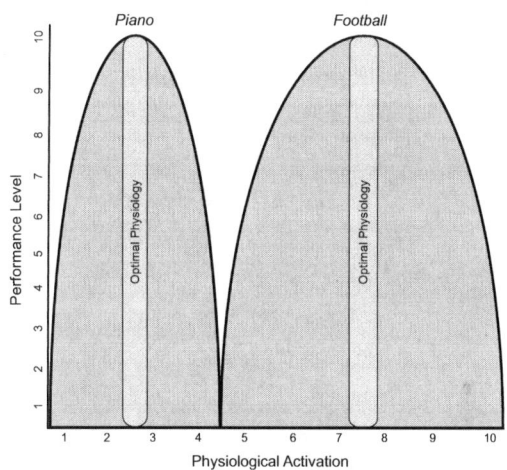

MANAGING ANXIETY

Eliminating anxiety altogether should not be your goal leading up to a performance. More often than not you will need to reduce your anxiety level while maintaing some level of physiological activation to perform your best. Sometimes even a little bit of activation or nervousness will make you feel uncomfortable. This is usually a good sign. Even today, after over twenty years of giving presentations to large groups, I pace around back stage asking, "Why do I do this to myself?" I feel all the discomfort of high expectations and the accompanying heightened physiology, such as, cold hands, shallow breathing, tension in my upper back and neck. The dread of forgetting parts of my presentation and the fears about the audience not liking what I say may add to my anxiety. I have learned these nervous feelings and thoughts are okay. They are simply a reminder or cue to psych myself down a bit, to remind myself it is the presence of this heightened physiology that provides much of the motivation for doing these presentations. It is what makes performance both challenging and rewarding!

When you manage your anxiety, there are times you will need to psych yourself down and times to psych yourself up. I sometimes experience the need to psych myself up when I teach class a few nights a week for fifteen weeks. For some class sessions, I feel a bit tired and the material is automatic. To "bring my 'A' game," I need to create additional excitement (trying something new or a little different) or attach some personal meaning (reminding myself these students have not heard the material before) to do my best or I will have a flat performance. Although managing your anxiety and activation level takes self-awareness and will power, it is not rocket science. If you are motivated to consistently perform your best, then learning to effectively manage your activation and anxiety levels is both necessary and attainable.

Understanding the specific causes of your anxiety leading up to a performance and then effectively managing your activation is an important part of creating a positive performance mindset.

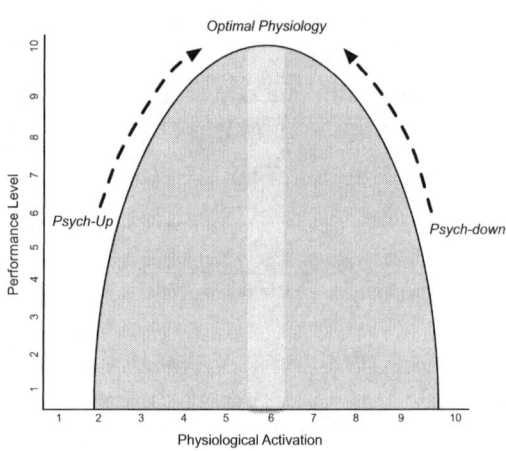

POSITIVE PERFORMANCE MINDSET

A positive performance mindset is a state of being calm and in control of yourself, yet excited about performing. It is important to understand this mindset is not all mental, but it is also physical and emotional. Your performance mindset is effected by your physical energy (e.g., rest, nutrition, body language), your emotional energy (e.g, excitement, fear), and your mental energy (e.g., alertness, attentional focus).

Mental energy is placed on a continuum from quiet to noisy. Clearing your thoughts or quieting your mind takes energy just as having many thoughts and a noisy mind takes energy. Harnessing your mental energy to quiet your mind so you can process information accurately and efficiently is an important aspect of a positive performance mindset. The same is true for your emotional and physical energies.

Emotional energy lies on both a continuum of positive or negative, and a continuum of high or low, creating four quadrants (see figure). The high negative quadrant consists of both high negative emotional and physical energies and result in an agitated state with little self-control. This state is sometimes experienced in a practice environment when you are having difficulty completing a difficult section or making the same mistake over and over. On the other hand, the high positive quadrant consists of an energized state that often results in a more focused and positive approach to your activity. The low negative quadrant reflects feelings of being discouraged and may result in self-defeating statements and a further withdrawal of effort. Although much of the music you play will be performed from the low positive quadrant (calm, focused and relaxed), there will be times or even sections of your performance where you will need to shift quadrants to effectively communicate the feeling and emotion in the music. When you are composed and in a positive performance mindset, this shift in emotion will be done easily and in a timely manor. You can probably think of many occasions and performance settings where both high-positive and low-positive energies are desirable. Although there are very few performance situations benefiting from either high-negative

High Negative	**High Positive**
Angry	Invigorated
Anxious	Confident
Defensive	Challenged
Frustrated	Joyful
Low Negative	**Low Positive**
Doubtful	Attentive
Tentative	Focused
Hopeless	Relaxed
Defeated	Peaceful

or low-negative energy, there are times when negative emotion can be helpful in communicating the proper emotion.

High negative emotion may also be helpful in focusing your efforts and energies during practice. Becoming angry can provide the necessary energy needed to focus when experiencing a bored or lackadaisical effort during a practice. It has been my experience that most musicians benefit from taking a short break from practice when they become excessively negative or frustrated.

When you bring a particular mindset to a situation, either positive or negative, you are, in essence, bringing a type of emotional and physical energy that affects you and the people around you. You have experienced how someone else's positive mindset has energized a group of people. A mindset consisting of high positive and high physical energy can be very infectious in some ensemble situations. The same can be said for a mindset consisting of high negative and low physical energy (e.g., someone who complains a lot but does not seek any solutions). Not only are they doing themselves a disservice, but they also bring down the other members of the group.

PERFORMANCE MINDSET MODEL

Being positive, confident, and in control of yourself before and during a performance is the cornerstone of a positive performance mindset. The performance mindset model describes a process consisting of five interrelated stages used to create either a positive or negative performance mindset. The stages in this model are: 1. Performance situation, 2. Perceived threats, 3. Physiological response, 4. Coping strategy, and 5. Performance mindset. Below is a brief description of these individual stages and how they relate to each other.

Stage 1: Performance Situation

The first stage in creating a performance mindset involves your perception of the performance demands and the value you place on doing well in the particular performance situation. In other words, whenever you enter into a performance situation, you have some understanding or perception of, how technically demanding or musically difficult the performance will be. The more demanding the performance piece, the greater potential for mistakes and the more

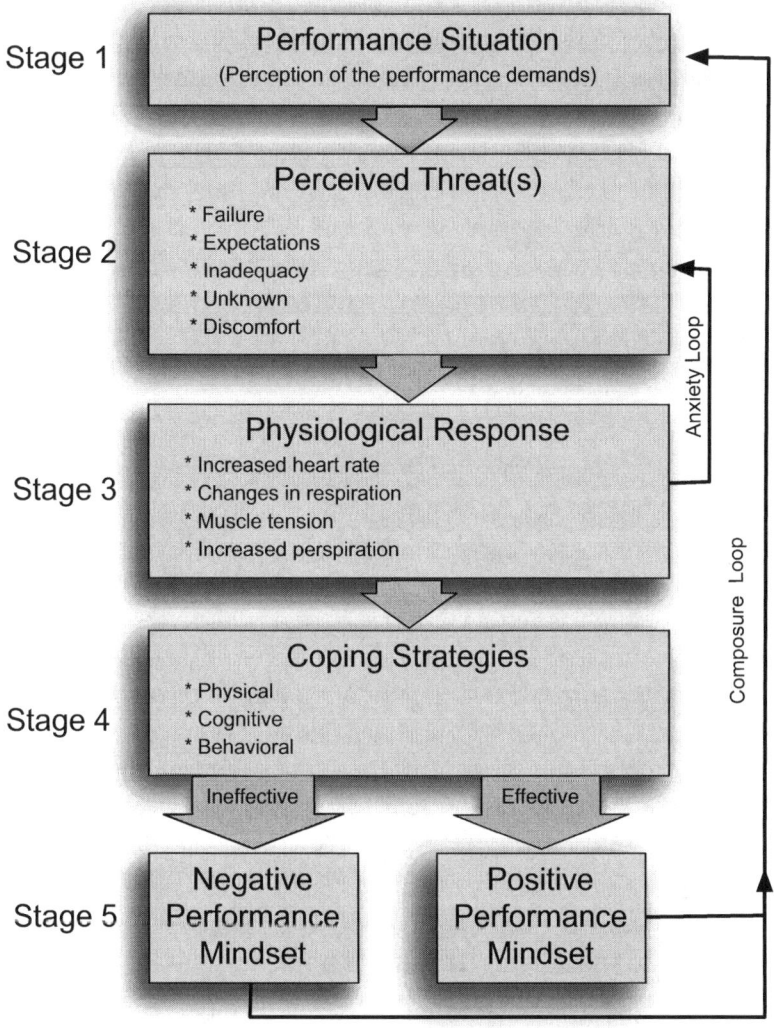

preparation and effort you will need to invest. You will make a determination of how important it is to you, to others, or both, that you perform well. For example, when performing an audition, during juries, or when in a competition, your perception of the importance of playing well is much higher than when playing for friends who just happened to stop by your house.

Although, your perception of the difficulty and the importance of your performance may or may not be accurate, it is still your perception that dictates your anxiety level, not necessarily the reality. You are hardwired to experience some level of heightened anxiety whenever you are evaluated. However, when you care deeply about doing well, especially when entering into a demanding situation, your anxiety increases even more. Usually, the greater the perceived importance of playing well, the greater the perceived consequences of failure. Therefore, it is not the performance situation in itself causing heightened anxiety, but your perception of both the performance situation and perceived consequences of failure. How effective you are in managing your thoughts and emotions will ultimately determine your mindset leading up to a performance.

Stage 2: Perceived Threats

A perceived threat is your perception of the possibility or likelihood that a negative consequence will occur as a result of a poor performance. Negative consequences can be personal, physical, or social. You may experience a personal threat when you believe a poor performance would reflect negatively on your ability as a musician (not meeting your own expectations) or a social threat, you believe a poor performance would let others down (not meeting others expectations). Occasionally, you might experience the physical threat of pain due to a chronic injury. Not all musicians perceive the same consequences or experience the same type or level of threat regarding their performance. For instance, two flutist's may perceive performing in their studio class quite differently. One flutist may have few aspirations or concern for playing well and looks forward to the enjoyment of being the center of attention. The other flutist, who has worked hard to improve, may feel threatened by the possibility of performing poorly and looking bad.

I have found the most common threats causing anxiety in musicians are: the threat of failure (fear of not performing up to standards), the threat of imposed expectations (fear of disappointing self or others), the threat of inadequacy, (fear of not being prepared), the threat of the unknown (fear of what might happen), and the threat of physical discomfort (fear of physical pain or inability to manage anxiety). Strategies for managing each of these threats are discussed in greater detail later in this chapter.

Stage 3: Physiological Response

The cognitive or evaluative aspect of anxiety is interrelated with the physiological aspect of the anxiety process. In other words, as you think anxious thoughts, your physiology becomes heightened and this heightened physiology validates your anxious thoughts. For example, if you are sitting in class and your teacher calls on students to answer questions aloud from a chapter you have not read, your thoughts of being called upon by your teacher (in front of your peers) and the potential embarrassment of an incorrect answer, cause your palms to sweat and your heart rate and breathing to increase. Your sweaty palms and accompanying physiology confirm you are unprepared and anxious which, in turn, causes more negative and distracting thoughts. This ratchets up your physiological response another notch.

When managing your anxiety before a performance, it is important to deal effectively with both your thoughts and your physiology. It is well documented that excess anxiety results in increased muscle tension and decreased attentional control, ultimately leading to performance decrements. Most top musicians are adept at detecting very subtle increases in anxiety and make the necessary adjustments. They can sense the extra tension in the shoulder and neck area or thought patterns that will inhibit their natural sense of rhythm and timing when playing. The effectiveness of your coping response dictates the level or severity of the physiology you experience. If you perceive you are "in over your head," that you are not adequately prepared for the demands of your performance, you will experience changes or increases in your physiology (e.g., cold clammy hands, rapid heart rate, shallow breathing). What you do about these changes, and how effective you are in getting them under control, will greatly affect your mindset going into your performance.

Stage 4: Coping Strategies

There are many different coping strategies used to reduce or manage anxiety and you will find some strategies more helpful than others. Although some overlap exists between these strategies, it is helpful to create a "menu" you may draw from to effectively manage your anxiety. The coping strategies are divided into three categories:

Physical or muscle-to-mind strategies (e.g., deep breathing, progressive relaxation), cognitive or mind-to-muscle strategies (e.g., meditation, affirmations, and visualization), and behavioral strategies (e.g., executing a pre-performance game plan, engaging in a diversion or distraction).

Stage 5: Performance Mindset

The fourth stage is your performance mindset. When you think of a musician who exhibits an effective performance mindset, clearly they bring a type of positive emotion and relaxed focus to what they are doing. If your performance mindset is dictated by your perception of the performance situation, you are in trouble. In other words, you must learn to create a positive performance mindset regardless of the situation in which you will be performing. The same can be said regarding how well or poorly you are playing during your performance. If you are positive, focused and confident when playing well and negative, distracted and doubtful when doing poorly, you will struggle with performing your best when it counts. Ideally, it is your mindset that should dictate your performance level, not your performance dictating your mindset. Sometimes musicians, as well as athletes, let their performance dictate their mindset. They begin performing with a positive mindset, then make a few mistakes, and their mindset becomes negative, instructive and fearful of further mistakes.

A performance mindset is a trusting and accepting mindset. It is the gateway to becoming totally absorbed in, and connected to, the music you are performing. You are in your performance mindset when you are free from expectations, fear of making mistakes, doubts about correctness of your technique, or other cognitive activities that keep you from fully expressing the feeling and emotion in your music. A positive performance mindset results from effectively managing your thoughts and emotions (perceived threats), and your physiology (coping response), not by focusing on what you do not have direct control over, such as the quality of your performance.

A negative performance mindset results from ineffectively managing your thoughts, emotions and physiology. If you are to perform optimally, there are situations where you need to change a negative mindset and create a positive mindset on demand. This is a skill you can practice in many areas of your life and apply to your music performance.

Whenever you engage your energies to complete a task, you are creating a mindset. The question is, "Are you in the proper mindset to be effective in what you are doing?" This takes self-awareness, discipline and willpower. Your mindset does not have to be dictated by your situation or your task. It is up to you. The following are strategies you can use to effectively manage your thoughts, emotions and physiology. This is an integral part of performing your best when it counts.

COPING STRATEGIES

Below is a description of various strategies you can choose from to create the most effective coping response(s) for you. I suggest trying the ones you think will make the biggest difference in your ability to create a positive performance mindset.

Physical Strategies (Muscle-to-Mind)

Muscle-to-mind strategies operate on the premise that relaxing your body and decreasing muscular tension is the first step in reducing your anxiety. It is important to first get your physiology under control, or within a manageable range, before you address the cognitive aspect of your anxiety.

Deep Breathing: One of the easiest and most effective ways to control your physiology and reduce muscle tension is through proper breathing. The pattern and depth of your breathing is typically quite different when you are calm and relaxed compared to when you are nervous and anxious. When you are calm and in control, your breathing is likely to be smooth, deep and rhythmical. When you are anxious your breathing tends to be short, shallow and irregular. One of the most common mistakes for musicians when they become anxious during a performance is to hold their breath or breathe improperly. Like other performance skills, proper breathing must be practiced. There is much material written on the efficacy of breath control during musical performance. This literature suggests breathing from the diaphragm instead of the chest produces a greater sense of mental and physical stability. In a practical sense, breath control can be used effectively during performance by scripting a deep breath at specific places during your performance (see focus plans).

A simple deep breathing technique is to count to seven while inhaling through your nose and filling your abdomen with air, much like you fill a pitcher of water, from bottom to top. Then exhale through your mouth as you count to three, emptying your abdomen of air from top to bottom. If you take five to ten deep breaths, you will immediately notice your physiology settling down and can begin to work on your thoughts to bring them more in line with a positive performance mindset.

Progressive Relaxation: Progressive relaxation techniques developed by Dr. Edmond Jacobson involve tensing and then relaxing specific muscles in order to develop an awareness of the difference between tension and relaxation. This is called progressive relaxation because you progress from one muscle group (e.g., hands and arms) to the next (e.g., shoulders, neck and face) until all muscle groups are relaxed. Start by tensing your facial muscles, inducing as mush tension as possible, feeling the tension for the count of 10. Then relax those muscles completely and move on to your neck and shoulders. By practicing progressive relaxation, you become skilled at recognizing tension in specific muscle groups, like the face, shoulders and neck, and releasing this tension on command.

There are a number of books and CD's you can buy that will take you through a progressive relaxation session. These sessions usually last from 20 to 40 minutes depending on the number of muscle groups covered. Obviously, a progressive relaxation session is not something you would want to do immediately before a performance since you would most likely be too relaxed to perform well. You may practice progressive relaxation a few times a week to enhance your ability to detect when you are excessively tense or anxious and release that tension very quickly and effectively.

Cognitive Strategies (Mind-to-Muscle)

Cognitive strategies are used to assist you in creating a frame of mind that is positive, committed and concentrative. Along with self-statements and images, these strategies can be used to affirm a positive belief and can also be used to clear your mind of excessive or negative thoughts.

Affirmations: Affirmations are positive self-statements that can be used in conjunction with relaxation strategies. You can combine the statement, *"Let it go"* as you exhale during deep breathing facilitating muscle tension leaving your body. You may find it helpful to us the affirmation, *"I am calm and relaxed"* as you take in each deep breath. Athletes use affirmations to instill positive beliefs about themselves and their performance. For example, a tennis player may repeat to herself during a match, "I am quick as a cat," to affirm her belief in her speed and agility as a player.

Affirmations are best used when you have thought through the specific feelings, actions or attitudes you need to result in your best performances. Once you make a list of these descriptors, you can choose the ones that provide the most meaning for your specific performance and develop a short statement to convey the meaning you want.

Visualization: Visualization is often referred to as mental imagery, or mental rehearsal, and is commonly used by musicians and athletes to create a calm, confident mindset before a performance. There are numerous examples throughout this book suggesting ways to use visualization to enhance your mental skills. Developing a performance script is an effective visualization strategy you can use to manage your anxiety and create a positive performance mindset.

Meditation: Meditation can be used to facilitate a state of deep relaxation and enhance your ability to detect negative or distracting thoughts and refocus. Most meditation techniques require three components: a quiet environment where you will not be disturbed, a comfortable sitting position you can hold for up to 20 minutes and a mantra or object to focus your attention (e.g., candle flame). A mantra is typically a two-syllable, nonsensical word that creates a rhythmical sound when repeated (e.g., I-ing). The benefits of meditation to overall health and happiness and human performance have been well documented.

Meditation helps you to gain control over your thoughts by teaching you how to recognize when thoughts appear and let them go without judging or attending to them. The ability to hold your attentional focus and refocus your attention when it drifts is fundamental to all human performance activities. Without a doubt, meditation enhances your ability to create a positive performance mindset; especially in today's fast paced, multitasking world where you do not often have the opportunity to practice these concentration and relaxation skills. Meditation is a practice. It takes disciple and desire to engage in meditation on a regular basis.

Behavioral Strategies

Behavioral strategies are actions you take to increase your sense of preparedness or take your mind off an upcoming performance. Developing and implementing a pre-planned and thought out schedule of events leading up to a performance (game plan) can be very helpful in giving you a sense of control that can facilitate anxiety management. Additionally, planning and engaging in a diversion during the day of a performance, such as going to see a movie or spending leisure time with friends and family, can provide a needed mental and emotional break.

Implement a Game Plan: A game plan is a road map that leads you to your performance. It is a plan for the day that provides specific direction on how you will spend your time from when you wake in the morning to when you walk out on stage. Your plan is meant to provide a guideline to follow and should not be considered fixed. Although, you will map out the timeline for events leading up to your performance, you will most likely make some minor changes.

Engage in a Diversion: Another way to cope with pre-performance anxiety is to distract your mind or divert your attention away from the upcoming event. Diversion is a means of sidestepping anxiety temporarily. You know you are going to perform later but you are choosing to divert your attention away from this prospect and relax until you are ready to mentally prepare.

Diversions can take many forms. These include, going to see a movie, spending time with family, shopping with friends, needlepoint, or reading. If you do choose to see a movie you might want to have a good idea of the style and content before you sit down. I remember going to see a movie the night before I played in the finals of a tennis tournament. The movie was called "The Deer Hunter" which had nothing to do with being in the woods and everything to do with being a prisoner of war and having to play Russian roulette until somebody shot himself through the head. I walked out of that movie feeling twice as exhausted as when I walked in.

REFRAMING PERCEIVED THREATS

There are a number of potential perceived threats or negative consequences of failure you may experience going into a performance situation resulting in heightened anxiety. The first step in effectively dealing with your anxiety leading up to a performance is to identify the specific perceived threat and understand where it is coming from. Once you have identified the specific threat, or combination of threats, you can begin to develop and implement coping strategies. Sometimes simply labeling the cause of your anxiety can facilitate managing your response.

Along with labeling your threat, you may find it helpful to reframe your perspective regarding your performance. Reframing is the process of using a question or statement to shift your perspective, enabling you to view yourself, or your task from a different angle; an angle that broadens your perspective and opens your mind to better solutions or greater optimism. Similar to any new behavior, it takes time to get good at reframing and make it a habit. Once learned, reframing can be an effective skill for setting your mind on the proper course. The following are common perceived threats that cause anxiety in musicians with an accompanying reframing question or statement for each to help you adjust your attitude about that particular threat.

Threat of Failure

Music performances typically do not have a final score at the end to determine a winner (unless being judged or graded) but this does not prevent musicians from fearing failure before a performance. I have found the fear of failure to be one of the most prevalent causes of performance anxiety across domains (e.g., sport, business, performing arts).

Fear of failure may take the form of an immediate fear of losing a competition, receiving a failing grade, making mistakes, or not connecting with the audience. Often it is the fear of failure that results in musicians playing not to make a mistake. As you likely have experienced, when you play not to fail you only increase the likelihood of making mistakes. Focusing intently on not failing will usually result in your performance lacking musicality, detracting from your enjoyment.

When you are experiencing self-doubts, fears, or the feelings of being overwhelmed, asking yourself, "*What am I afraid of?*" can help you reframe your perspective, identifying your negative feelings, and begin to get them under control. This reframing question points to a specific aspect of your fear that you may not have considered but might be holding you back. This probes you to consciously consider a specific feeling about your performance. By doing so you become more empowered to change your fear and therefore your approach to the situation. I direct a weekly Performance Club where musicians from a variety of disciplines come and perform in front of other musicians. Some pieces are works in progress while others are recital ready. I often hear from the performers, it is less "stressful" to perform in front of an audience of musicians who do not play the same instrument than it is to play for a studio class where every one knows the music and knows when you make a mistake. Once these musicians become aware of their specific fears or self-doubts that spark their anxiety, they can begin to adjust their attitude and reframe perspective.

Threat of Imposed Expectations

As an increase in time, energy and money are invested into your performance outcomes, either by yourself or by others (e.g., parents, teachers), you will experience an increase in expectations regarding the quality of your performance. Similar to the fear of failure, the threat of heightened expectations is a fear of the perceived negative consequences associated with not meeting expectations of yourself and/or others. This fear can be especially anxiety producing if you feel the expectations exceed your ability to meet them.

The fear of not meeting expectations is common in musicians who want to please their parents or instructor and is especially prevalent in musicians who are perfectionistic. In both cases, the margin of error is very small as is the likelihood of meeting or exceeding the expectation. The threat of heightened expectations and fear of the accompanying negative consequences is often learned early in a musicians development. As adults invest more time and money, a young musician experiences an increase in expectations, regardless of how often or sincere these adults are in communicating just 'do your best' or 'have fun.' Similarly, there is an increase in expectations from yourself and others, as you become a more skilled musician and better performer. The fear of not meeting expectations is a very real fear for many musicians and is often a factor in heightened anxiety.

Although you may never eliminate expectations, you can make them more manageable and less anxiety provoking. Heightened expectations often cause us to overgeneralize the negative consequences of failure. Sometimes asking, *"What is the worst thing that can happen?"* will help you reframe your fears and doubts into a more narrow perspective. You realize you are capable of handling the worst possible outcome in this situation. It is just not that bad! There is *always* something worse that can happen to you outside of this particular performance situation. Once you have minimized the fear, you can begin to muster up the courage to act in the face of your fear. In the previous example, the worst thing that could happen was your expert audience in your studio class was critical of that particular performance. Such a consequence might initially be emotionally difficult, especially if your self-worth is tied to how others judge your performance, but it is not the worst thing that could happen, right?

Threat of Inadequacy

The fear you are not adequately prepared for an upcoming event can be characterized by a personal dissatisfaction with your preparation, a feeling something is just wrong (e.g., not enough sleep, inability to control tension or anxiety), or a belief the challenge is greater than your level of competence. Whatever the factors causing your feelings if inadequacy, the result is feeling anxious because you do not believe you have what it takes to meet the performance challenge.

There are a surprisingly high number of performers who are insecure about their own success and fear each time they perform the "curtain will be pulled" and others will discover the Wizard of OZ is just an ordinary person with ordinary talent. Although this fear often provides a great deal of motivation to work harder, it can sometimes become debilitating before a performance. This particular fear leading up to a performance is synonymous to what might be called the imposture syndrome. This is the fear you will be found out, that others will discover you are not as good as they thought, and this realization will be devastating. The fear of being inadequate is sometimes magnified by the perception your personal worth or esteem is tied to your performance outcomes. This means good performances bolster your personal value and bad performances detract from it. Although there are a host of problems when you tie your self-esteem to performance outcomes, one common result is not taking the chances often needed to grow as a musician and performer, not risking the possibility of failure by putting yourself in a challenging performance situation. In both cases you are choosing to play it safe and not push yourself to grow.

As a parent, I take great pride in the fact my oldest son, Brennan, is able to risk and even embrace failure. This one characteristic has propelled him to accomplish things I would have never believed possible for him. The existence of this wonderful trait first became apparent to me when he was learning to waterski one summer. There were a number of friends and family in the boat and Brennan was the only one who could not get up on his skis. He kept falling and trying and falling again. I started to get embarrassed for him but each time we brought the boat around to pick him up he was laughing and making silly comments about his athleticism, or lack there of. The truth is, his failures, and his inadequacies, did not phase him one bit! He has since gone on to receive a scholarship at the North Carolina School of Arts, then Tuffs University and is currently combining his art background with mathematics in a graduate program at MIT. This is a child whom I nicknamed "OB" for oblivious because he would literally walk into walls as a teenager.

Take a moment to reflect upon how you deal with your own inadequacies. Can you embrace them or occasionally laugh at them? How would your life be different if you were able to risk failure, try new things, put yourself on the line, and not take failure personally? We all have inadequacies and we all fail. The key is to not become obsessed with our inadequacies and failures to the point where they keep us from pushing our limits.

Your inadequacies do not make up who you are, they are part of you. You can either choose to focus on what is missing in your life, or your skill set, or you can focus on what you have, your gifts and strengths. One way to reframe your perspective is to ask yourself, *"How am I fortunate?"* This is a good reframing question to use whenever you are feeling overwhelmed with thoughts of inadequacy or feeling the pressure to perform beyond your perceived limits. Often we take for granted the blessings and gifts we have been given. Focusing on how you are fortunate is not meant to make you feel guilty (e.g., "Think of the starving children who would love to be as fortunate as you") but instead to feel thankful (e.g., "How many other people have the opportunity to do what they love to do in front of an audience like I do?"). Though the fear of inadequacy may be based in your perceived competence, it is not grounded in your overall belief of your true capabilities. It is simply a fear that you may not have what it takes to be successful, today. Do not let this fear dictate your choices effecting you in the future.

Threat of the Unknown

Whenever you perform there are many unknowns. You honestly do not know if you will play well, connect with the audience, or be successful. This is what makes performing so exciting! Often musicians must enter into performances where there are a greater degree of unknown variables than they are accustom to. These unknown variables or factors could be: environmental (venue temperature or sound quality), relational (unfamiliar ensemble members), physical (pain from previous injury), technical (difficult section), or psychological (memorization). It usually is not just the unknown aspect causing anxiety but the perception of your ability to effectively adjust to the unknown that causes anxiety.

I once worked with a pianist who was traveling across country to perform in New York in front of a large audience. Her plane was delayed over night in Chicago and arrived shortly before she was to perform. The piano was not what she expected and the auditorium was very large. Instead of panicking she reframed her perspective by repeating the question, *"How can I make this an adventure?"* This perspective allowed her to shift her focus from the unexpected problems and negative events that occurred to focusing on solutions.

If you have the opportunity to perform in a variety of places over an extended time, one thing you will learn is to "expect nothing but be ready for anything." Rarely do all things fall into place perfectly before, during and after a performance. Learning how to go with the flow and not panic or be thrown off-kilter when the unexpected happens is critical to a long and happy career. Next time things get a little wacky ask yourself, *"How can I make this an adventure?"* This will free you up to take whatever is thrown your way and run with it.

Threat of Physiological Discomfort

Sometimes the fear of the physiological manifestations of anxiety can cause greater anxiety. If you have had bad experiences with performance anxiety in the past, the sensations you experience pre-performance can trigger a heightened anxiety response. Some of these sensations may include;:rapid heart rate, upset stomach, shaking or trembling, feeling cold or stiff, sweating, excessive yawing, rapid, shallow breathing, dizziness and dry mouth. This physiological discomfort can cause you to think about the negative effects these feelings will have on your performance which will magnify the anxiety response. To break this downward spiral, you will need to reframe your perspective of the situation.

One way to reframe your perspective and begin to get your physiology under control is to ask yourself, *"How is this situation an opportunity?"* You can find some opportunity in almost every situation. By reframing an anxiety producing event into an opportunity, you become more focused on a solution rather than on the problem. Once you become more solution-focused you will begin to see other possibilities that keep you moving forward. For example; you have been asked unexpectedly to fill-in for a fellow performer at the last minute with little preparation. You can choose to focus on your lack of preparation (resulting in heightened anxiety) or use this as an opportunity to test your mental toughness, your ability to adjust "on the fly," or your creative skills. By choosing to reframe your perspective, you focus on how to make it work rather than how bad or inconvenient it is. As a result, you will get your physiology under control.

CREATING A POSITIVE PERFORMANCE MINDSET

The steps for creating a positive performance mindset for a musical performance is similar to other performances that require you to prepare in advance, harness your emotional energy, and focus intensely (e.g., taking a test, job interview). Music performances are also unique because of the perceived consequences of failure, the small margin for error, and the heightened physiology that accompany this evaluative situation. Below are three steps you can complete for creating a positive performance mindset for your musical performances: 1) Reframe your performance threat, 2) Get your physiology under control, and 3) Use performance based affirmations. Take the time to review the steps below and reflect upon how you can best use them to create a positive performance mindset.

Step 1: Reframe Your Performance Threat

The first step in creating a positive performance mindset is to understand and even embrace your *specific* fears or perceived threats regarding your performance. Musicians generalize their feelings when they say, "I get really nervous before I play," and leave it at that without going a little deeper to understand what is it about performing that is causing their anxiety. Often you will find it helpful to define your specific fears so you can begin to understand and then reframe them.

Sometimes creating a positive performance mindset is only half of the battle. Changing a negative performance mindset is the other half and is just as important and difficult to do. Perhaps some of the things you have done before have worked in reframing or changing a negative mindset. You can use additional tools, particularly when hit by an especially persistent and negative mindset. Often when you start down a path of negative thinking, your perspective becomes very narrow and focused on the negative. Gaining a different perspective or reframing the situation can help you to quickly flip your attitude.

Changing a negative mindset or response to a particular situation can be very challenging and requires a great deal of self-awareness and desire to do so. Being able to adjust your mindset on command is a skill you can learn and develop through practice. Think of how often such a skill would have affected your past approaches and responses to everyday situations. You can control your mindset and develop new and more effective ways of responding to negative and stressful events both in your life and your performances. Start by getting more specific with what is causing you to be negative or anxious and then use reframing questions to provide the fresh perspective needed to harness energy to change it.

Step 2: Get Your Physiology Under Control

Once you have interrupted or stopped the negative cycle by reframing your fear, you can begin to get your physiology under control. This allows you to engage in the more effective thinking necessary for creating a positive performance mindset. This is best done using the two physical or muscle-to-mind strategies previously discussed in this chapter: deep breathing and progressive relaxation. If you have a pattern of experiencing excessive anxiety, I suggest you make a habit of regularly practicing either progressive relaxation or meditation. These techniques will provide you with the awareness needed to detect changes in your physiology and the skills to reduce these effects very quickly. On the other hand, if you feel your primary goal is to lower your physiological response so you can better manage your thoughts and keep your emotions within an acceptable range, deep breathing should be sufficient. Once your physiology is within an acceptable range, you can begin to address your cognitions as a means of getting your mind ready to play your best.

Step 3: Use Performance Based Affirmations

Performance based affirmations are words or statements that act as either a positive reminder or a refocus instruction you repeat to yourself before and/or during a performance. Often it is helpful to write the affirmation on a piece of tape, and it somewhere you can see it, and refer to it during performances. For example, a basketball player came to me with the specific problem of becoming excessively frustrated during practices and games whenever he made a mistake. This caused him to loose focus on the next possession, often resulting in another mistake or poor play. Although his coach was patient he finally sat the player on the bench because his emotional displays were both an embarrassment to the team and the player. In trying to develop a performance-based affirmation to help the player refocus after a mistake, the player and I discussed three affirmations: refocus, rebound and let-go. We then assessed which one would have the most meaning regarding the goal of letting go of the mistake and refocusing on the next play. The player chose the word, "Rebound," as his affirmation to mentally and emotionally rebound after a poor play or mistake. To drive this point home, I taped the word to the toe of each shoe and both his wrists during practice. After a few practice session she was able to put a piece of tape around his index finger with the letter "R" as a physical reminder of his performance affirmation. Each time he made a mistake he would look at the tape on his finger and remember to rebound and get ready for the next possession.

POSTSCRIPT

When you think of performance as, "any time you must harness your energy and focus to complete a task," you can see that you are performing throughout the day and under a variety of conditions. This is good news in that you are provided with a number of opportunities or repetitions for recognizing your current mindset and then having the presence of mind to either maintain that mindset or change it to one that is more effective. Whether you are driving in traffic, listening to your significant other, or pushing yourself in practice, you are in a performance mindset because each example requires you to engage your energy and focus to be successful. Creating the proper mindset does not always mean you have to muster a positive high energy state. It may simply mean that you *get your head ready* to do what you need to do.

As a motivated performer, you are not only expected to effectively manage competing demands on your time and the internal and external pressures to perform great, but you must also muster the positive energy and effort required for daily practices and be able to create a positive performance mindset on demand. The higher your anxiety, the more difficult it is to create the mindset you desire. Creating a positive performance mindset on demand can be tough indeed! However, keep in mind, whether you find yourself in a positive or in a negative mindset, you have *created* it.

Creating a positive performance mindset begins with recognizing your ability to control your thoughts and physiology. By increasing your awareness of typical or habitual responses working against a positive mindset, you will begin to proactively create the kind of mindset you need to perform your best and perform your best more consistently.

SELF-REFLECTION QUESTIONS

1. In the space below, write down three challenging, fearful, or overwhelming situations you are facing or are likely to face. Identify the specific perceived threat and reframe your perspective using a different reframing response (e.g., Situation: Entering an audition room and noticing excellent talent. Perceived threat: Fear of failure and not meeting expectations. Reframing response: Remember my shirt message, "I belong here. What I have is good enough."

Situation	Perceived Threat	Reframing Response

2. Think about the sources of stress (persons, situations, demands, fears, etc.) causing you to feel up tight, anxious and nervous. How do these things both enhance and detract from your performances and life quality? How might you better manage the negative stressors in your life? What are some specific ways you can control the stress in your life?

_____
_____
_____
_____
_____
_____
_____
_____
_____

3. To better understand your stress response, check the responses you experience when stressed and when each responses occur (B=before, D=during). Also, indicate any other responses not listed.

____ B ____ D   Tired arms and legs

____ B ____ D   Groggy and heavy feeling

____ B ____ D   Rapid & noticeable heartbeat

____ B ____ D   Rapid breathing

____ B ____ D   Butterflies in your stomach

____ B ____ D   Need to urinate

____ B ____ D   Excessive perspiration

____ B ____ D   Headaches

____ B ____ D   Tight muscles

____ B ____ D   Anxiousness, nervousness

____ B ____ D   Dry mouth

____ B ____ D   Fatigue

____ B ____ D   _____

____ B ____ D   _____

____ B ____ D   _____

____ B ____ D   _____

7
Designing Your Performance Future

The Fox Who Lost His Tail

A fox caught in a trap, escaped by tearing off his brushy tail. After that, the other animals mocked him, making him feel so ashamed that his life was a burden to him. He therefore worked out a plan to make all the other foxes the same as him, so in their common loss he might better conceal his own deprivation.

He called a meeting of the foxes. A good many came to it, and he gave a speech, advising them all to cut off their tails. He said they would not only look better without them, but they would get rid of the weight of the brush, which was a great inconvenience.

One of them interrupted his speech. "If you had not lost your own tail, my friend," that fox said, "you would not be giving us this advice."

Accomplishing challenging and lofty goals requires committing to a path you have chosen while overcoming difficult obstacles along the way. You will meet many people in your life who have stopped pursuing their dreams of becoming a great performer in music, sports, or some other profession. For whatever reason, they stopped believing they could make their dreams come true and stopped doing what it took to realize them. Often, it is these people who, like the fox, want you to share their "loss" by persuading you to give up your dreams.

Many people have lost their dreams along the road to success and turned back. There is no doubt your road to performance excellence is full of potholes and speed bumps testing your ability to stay on course. Many musicians also get stuck along the way; unable or unwilling to try something different to keep on the right path or even to keep going. Some are trapped in a pursuit of excellence without balance in their lives, meaning in their relationships, or purpose in their vision. They are running hard to get through the day without a clear destination of where they are going or why they are trying to get there.

Leadership starts with a goal or vision; whether you are leading yourself or leading others, you must first have a clear understanding of where you want to go. Although self-leadership begins with creating a goal for the future, it does not end there. Your goal must also have a purpose. Without a purpose or reason for accomplishing your goal, it is easy to lose the focus and determination necessary to stay the course when facing the many distractions and challenges along the way. If your reasons for pursuing your goals are not connected to, or consistent with, the values you hold dear, you will wake someday unhappy with where you are and wondering how you got so far off track. Even if you have given yourself, your goals, your life's destination over to a higher power, you are still responsible to seek them with passion and purpose. This can be very challenging in a work environment which involves long hours and many competing demands. It is easy to get caught up in day-to-day tasks and immediate distractions without taking time to truly reflect upon *where* you are going and *why* you are striving to get there.

Realizing your dream is your responsibility. You are the director and designer of your performance future. Your goals are a function of your decisions, not a function of your conditions. Becoming a great self-leader means you regularly revisit your core values, your goals, and reasons for doing what you do. Self-leadership requires moments of quiet time required to clarify your vision and create the future you desire.

Many people would say there is no better feeling in the world than to know they battled toward their dream and gave it everything they had. It is satisfying to stand at the end of a road, the end of the year, or the end of a career, and look back, knowing it was all worth it! While you are never guaranteed your commitment will result in the outcome you desire, you are guaranteed if your goals are lofty, you will not achieve them without the thoughtful reflection and personal commitment found in self-leadership.

SELF-LEADERSHIP

Why is it that two musicians with nearly identical mental and physical capabilities reach two entirely different levels of performance? What separates them? Why does one accomplish his goals while the other does not? As a musician, you have many competing demands and distractions that challenge your ability to stay committed, confident, and focused during both practices and performances. Having the self-leadership skills to guide you toward a vision of your future, a vision you believe in and are committed to, is necessary to keeping you on track.

Given the multiple distractions, interruptions, and task demands you experience every day, effectively leading yourself is more important now than at any other time in your life. You must take control of your life if you want to achieve your performance goals while sustaining a degree of balance and effectiveness in your personal life. Choosing to take the necessary steps to lead yourself effectively is up to you. These steps involve mustering the courage to face your fears and self-doubts regarding accomplishing your dream goal, reflecting upon and connecting with what you value, and creating a vision for yourself that is consistent with these values. It takes quiet, uninterrupted time. In a world of mobile phones, multitasking, voice, and e-mails, it is almost an embarrassing reality that many of us feel too busy to take time to reflect upon what we want our future to look like and what we truly value in our lives.

Having a clear vision for your personal life can be helpful in recognizing and capitalizing on opportunities and making difficult life decisions (e.g., family, career, financial). A clear vision is necessary to achieving your dream goal as a musician, especially if performing music is a major category in your life requiring a large investment of your time and energy. You can have a goal as a performer that is separate and distinct from the big picture goal you have for your life. You might be at a stage of your life where creating a clear personal vision seems too daunting or irrelevant. Whether you have a clear personal vision or not, having a vivid picture of who you want to be and where you want to go as a musician is critical to sustaining the type of effort needed to be successful in achieving your performance goal. Clarifying and connecting with the reasons underlying why you want to accomplish your dream goal as a musician is important to the self-leadership process.

SELF-LEADERSHIP PROCESS

How would you describe the big picture goal, the dream goal you have for yourself as a musician? Can you describe it in detail? What does this picture look like? Certainly it is much easier to just 'go with the flow' and see where you end up in five or ten years. Think for a moment about how your decisions and actions would be different if you did have a clear picture of your future as a musician. A vivid image you reflected upon, revised, and revisited on a regular basis. I suggest two things would change. First, you will begin to see opportunities and meet people that keep you moving in the right direction, and second, belief in your ability to attain your goal would increase drastically.

Someone once said, *"All great accomplishments are created twice."* You must first have a mental creation, or vision, of what you want before you can realize a physical creation or the actual accomplishment. I would also add, there must be a level of belief you will achieve your goal. Accomplishing big goals is never easy; however, when you have a picture of the end in your mind, your belief in your ability to accomplish your goal will grow, affecting both the intensity and the persistence of your efforts in achieving that goal.

An effective self-leadership process involves the successful execution of five sequential steps. Although, these steps are applied specially to accomplishing your goal as a musician and performer, the same steps can be applied to any long-term goal, such as a vision for your career, a particular piece of music, or a project you want to complete (e.g., writing a book). The self-leadership steps for creating a performance future of your design are: 1. Clarify your core performance values, 2. Identify your performance vision, 3. Embrace your performance vision, 4. Anticipate barriers to your vision, and 5. Write your performance mission statement. Reflect upon your own goals and aspirations as a musician as you read through these steps.

1. Clarify Core Performance Values

What are the core values guiding you in the performance of your craft? These are values you strive to live up to regardless of your situation. Core performance values provide you with a code of conduct for your journey through excellence. They have worth in and of themselves and, when reflected upon, can provide a source of inspiration and meaning to your pursuit of excellence. They guide your actions both in practice and during performance. You do not change them, even if your conditions change. The first step in creating your core performance values is to capture what you authentically believe, not what others value or what society thinks you should value. Although there are commonly recognized universal values such as integrity, generosity, courage, humility, compassion, loyalty, and perseverance, these may not be the core values most compelling to you as a performer.

In the box below, circle or write all the values you hold as a musician. Within the box is a partial list that might help stimulate your thinking. Feel free to generate your own performance values. After you have circled or developed your own values, go through the list and write down your four or five most meaningful, or most compelling performance values and describe what each one means to you (e.g., Respect: a respect for the music, the people creating it, the composers and the audience)

Authenticity	Balance	Competence	Commitment	Compassion
Connection	Courage	Competitiveness	Creativity	Challenge
Drive	Dedication	Discipline	Empathy	Excellence
Faithfulness	Family	Freedom	Friendship	Expression
Generosity	Genuine	Greatness	Happiness	Harmony
Health	Humor	Integrity	Fun	Independence
Knowledge	Mastery	Toughness	Openness	Perseverance
Respect	Responsibility	Recognition	Service to others	Serenity
Sincerity	Sharing			

_____   _____
_____   _____

	Performance Values	What the value means to me
1		
2		
3		
4		
5		

How do these core values express themselves during your performances? Are you currently performing and practicing according to these values? Are there gaps between how you would like to be and how you actually are? At this time, stop reading and complete the first Self-reflection Question located at the end of this chapter. This activity will expand your understanding of what you value as a musician and performer.

2. Identify Your Performance Vision

Ask yourself, "When I let go of all fears and self-doubts, what vision do I have of myself as a performer that truly excites me?" What image inspires you so much that you are willing to commit yourself wholeheartedly toward its realization? It may not seem possible from where you sit today. You probably have some ideas and you may even have a clear answer to that question. It is important you take some time to really think about what is truly possible for you. What is possible if you become passionately committed to a vision of yourself as a performer?

Take just few moments to put into words the picture of the future you desire as a performer. Be sure whatever you come up with it is truly *your* goal and *your* vision. Describe your vision in detail with as much vivid images and language as you can.

My Performance Vision

4. Embrace Your Performance Vision

Your performance vision is an image that excites you; one you care about attaining and expands your belief in what is possible for you as a musician. The first step toward embracing your performance vision is to understand the *"why"* and the *"why not"* behind that goal. Why is this vision important to you? What are the reasons keeping you going? Start by thinking about the aspects of the vision that put a smile on your face: why you love it! Then begin to understand what this vision gives back to you.

A purpose for your goal not only helps to clarify your destination, it drives you toward it. Having a clear and vivid purpose answers a resounding "Yes" to the question, "Is the goal I am pursing worth what I am giving up to get it?" If your answer is "No," then you need to either change your goal or connect with a different purpose.

Pursuing any goal of value requires you to make sacrifices, to give certain things up, to accomplish it.

So why would you *not* want to make an honest commitment to your performance vision? What are the costs? There are probably more reasons not to pursue your goal than there are to pursue it: maybe because it is hard work or uncomfortable for you to truly believe in yourself, or it hurts more when you fail after caring about doing well, or because other people around you are not committed to their dream, or because others may not be supportive of your efforts. Maybe others will become jealous or maybe they do not want you to fail and get hurt. There are numerous reasons why you should not believe in yourself and your dreams. In fact, there are more reasons to do nothing than to do something! All you need is one great reason and, if you fall passionately in love with that one reason, then all the "why not's" will fall away. On the other hand, you may sincerely answer the question and realize there are too many important reasons against continuing. If so, you have saved time, energy, and heartache that would have been lost on a halfhearted or doomed effort. Perhaps you can modify your vision to eliminate enough of the "why-nots" to move ahead.

Your purpose provides you with reasons to keep going and to persist through difficult challenges necessary for achieving your goals. Take a minute and reflect upon why your vision is worth your time and energy. What will you gain from realizing this goal? What will achieving your vision give back to you?

Why my vision is important to me
_____
_____
_____
_____

Now that you have a better understanding of why you want to pursue your vision, think through some of the reasons as to *why not* - why you might not want to pursue your goal. This process can help you determine if the goal is really something you are invested in pursuing, and can help you build your own intrinsic motivation for going for it. Take a minute and reflect on why you would *not* want to make an honest commitment to your goal? What are the costs? What are the reasons why you should not believe in yourself and pursue your performance vision?

The costs of committing to my vision

4. Anticipate Mental Barriers

Having willpower driving you toward your goal is only half of the total picture. You must also have the way-power needed to overcome obstacles. You probably know people who seem highly motivated but, once they meet an obstacle to their goal, they stop pursuing it without looking for a way around the barrier. You will always find obstacles in your path toward lofty goals. Some you can push through with sheer willpower, but others, you must develop and implement strategies for going around or finding alternate routes. Take a moment to think about mental barriers you will face when fully committing to your performance vision. Identify four that stand out as barriers that must be overcome to achieve your goal (e.g., poor time management, fear of failure, fear of job security)

Mental Barrier 1:
Mental Barrier 2:
Mental Barrier 3:
Mental Barrier 4:

5. Write a Performance Mission Statement

Keeping your dream alive is paramount to achieving it. You breathe life into your dream every time you look at it on paper or see it in your mind's eye. By keeping your dream visible, you allow it to pull you in the right direction. When you keep your performance vision or dream in the forefront of your mind, you see opportunities that you would not see otherwise. For example, let's say you are serious about buying a new car, a red Ford Mustang. Now, when you drive around town, you notice more red cars and especially Ford Mustangs. They were there all along but you did not notice them. Once you became interested in buying this car, and had it in the front of your mind, you saw something that was there all along but did not attend to – all the other red cars and other Mustangs. The same is true when you become serious about a goal and keep it in your mind. There are opportunities and individuals that were there all along, but only now you see them. Creating your performance mission statement is part of creating a performance future of your design. Your mission statement should inspire you and provide direction and guidance.

POSTSCRIPT

The pace of life today is unlike any other time in human history. Never before have human beings been required to respond to the number, or the complexity, of demands and at the speeds they do today. Many people, maybe even you, are choosing to live their lives by simply reacting to the forces that pull them in different directions everyday, in essence, living their lives by default, not by design. Living by default allows important situations, urgent tasks, and the will of others, to dictate what you do, and when you do it.

If you feel like you are being pushed to your absolute limit just to get through the day and you felt the same way a year ago, what do you expect will be different next year? If you are putting in the time to become a better musician, but are not sure where you are headed, at what point will you decide to get on a path that leads to a destination of your choosing? Self-leadership is taking responsibility to get where you want to go, both as a person and as a musician. Leading yourself means that you choose to act first, you determine where you are going, you create the vision for yourself as a musician, and you are proactive in doing the things you need to do to realize your vision. For some, it is difficult to accept they are where they are today largely because of the choices they made yesterday. Until you truly embrace the reality that your future as a musician and a performer is in large part, your responsibility, you will continue to react and respond to the forces pulling you into the urgent and immediate, without any connection to a future, with meaning and passion.

SELF-REFLECTION QUESTIONS

1. In your mind's eye, see yourself going to the retirement party of a close friend. Picture yourself driving to the gathering. You walk down to the front of the room and take a seat at your table. As you wait for the service to begin, you look at the program in your hand and realize this is your retirement party. All the people present have come to your party to honor your accomplishments and express feelings of love and appreciation for you as a musician. There are to be four speakers. The first is from your family (parent, sibling, grandparent), someone who can talk about what you loved about performing music as a child. The second speaker is your best friends or your significant other, someone who can give a sense of what performing music meant to you as an adult. The third is a classmate or band member who can talk about what you were like as a fellow musician or ensemble member, and the fourth, your mentor or favorite teacher who will talk about you as a musician and performer. Now think deeply. *What would you like each of these speakers to say about you and your life as a musician?* What kind of musician would you like their words to reflect? What kind of performer would you like to be described as? What characteristics would you like them to have seen in you? What contributions and achievements would you want them to remember? Look carefully at the people around you. How would you like to be remembered as a musician?

Family member: _____

_____

_____

Friend/significant other: _____

_____

_____

Classmate/ensemble member: _____

_____

_____

Mentor/teacher: _____

_____

_____

2. Considering your responses to question one, what is the "one thing" that if you did on a regular basis would make the greatest positive difference in your performance future?

The One Thing
_____

3. Keep your performance mission statement in the front of your mind by writing it down and revisiting it. This will focus your thoughts and energy and enable you to take advantage of opportunities and deal successfully with unexpected distractions. It is best to display your mission statement where you can see it (e.g., on your bathroom mirror, note cards) so it can act as a constant reminder. In the space provided below create a *rough draft* of your performance mission statement. Draw heavily on

the thinking you've done in the previous activities. You may find it helpful to view the other mission statements provided at the end of this worksheet. Below are two examples of performance mission statements.

"My mission is to inspire others through my performances. I will strive to continually improve my skills and invent the future rather than being a victim of my past failures and mistakes. I will honor personal courage, creativity, independence, and personal integrity. I will frequently remind myself that, without risk, there is neither success nor failure, remembering the phrase, "If the primary mission of a captain were to preserve his ship, he would never leave port." Finally, I pledge myself to being a caring and honest friend to those around me and to always attempt to do what I say I will do."

"I will embrace each day as not just another day, but one filled with opportunity and excitement. I desire to perform with creativity, passion and courage. Being technically and musically correct are my priorities. I believe that if I remain true to my training, I will perform well and with conviction. I realize that I can always improve my skills and, with this in mind, I will consciously seek to understand and obtain greater knowledge and maturity as a performer. I will continue to grow as a performer by stimulating my mind with new learning and have the courage to try difficult challenges."

Mission Statement Draft
_____
_____
_____
_____
_____
_____
_____

8
Making It Happen

The Frog and the Scorpion

There once lived a scorpion and a frog. The scorpion wanted to cross the pond but, being a scorpion, he couldn't swim. So he scuttled up to the frog and asked: "Please, Mr. Frog, can you carry me across the pond on your back?"

"I would," replied the frog, "but, under the circumstances, I must refuse. You might sting me as I swim across." "But why would I do that?" asked the scorpion. "It is not in my interests to sting you, because you will die and then I will drown."

Although the frog knew how lethal scorpions were, the logic proved quite persuasive. Perhaps, felt the frog, in this one instance the scorpion would keep his tail in check. So the frog agreed. The scorpion climbed onto his back and together they set off across the pond. Just as they reached the middle of the pond, the scorpion twitched his tail and stung the frog.

Mortally wounded, the frog cried out: "Why did you sting me? It is not in your interests to sting me, because now I will die and you will drown."

"I know," replied the scorpion as he sank into the pond. "But I am a scorpion. I have to sting you. It's in my nature."

People often quit pursuing their goals for the same reason as the scorpion. They were unwilling to change some aspect of their nature at the expense of getting where they wanted to go. Have you ever heard someone push against the possibility of change by saying, "That's just the way I am" or "I've never done it that way before?" What changes are you willing to make to accomplish your ultimate goal? Most likely, you will need to make changes in your strategy and even your nature to get where you want to go. Accomplishing a challenging goal requires you to stay on a certain path despite competing demands and seemingly insurmountable obstacles. The scorpion gave into his nature because he lost sight of his true goal. He choose not display the discipline needed to reach his goal.

If self-leadership means designing your performance future, then self-management is "walking the walk" that gets you there. Self-management includes the goal attainment strategies necessary to accomplish your vision. It involves identifying and achieving the intermediate steps making up the staircase to your long-term performance goal, your daily and weekly management of the direction and intensity of your efforts. Making it happen not only depends on how well you manage your time, but also how well you manage your energy.

SELF-MANAGEMENT

People today work longer hours, get less sleep, and make more difficult decisions under greater pressure than ever before. As a result, many of us are struggling with a need for personal effectiveness, healthy relationships with others, and a connection to a greater purpose. Given the nature of today's demands, you cannot apply your parents self-management strategies to achieve both performance excellence and personal balance in your life.

Good self-managers recognize the relationship between an intense work environment and the need for effective time management skills, regular reenergizing activities, and an effective goal attainment plan. The goal of self-management is not to eliminate the daily stress in your life but to enhance your ability and capacity to handle your stress. Self-management is viewed as a process of engaging in strategies enabling you to perform at the upper range of your potential more consistently. Self-management is an ongoing process that genuinely connects you to your long-term performance goal on a weekly and monthly basis. The strategies for effective self-management include: self-renewal, time management and goal attainment.

SELF-RENEWAL

Imagine you come across someone working hard to saw down a tree. You notice how exhausted she is and ask, "How long have you been at it?" She replied, "Over five hours and I'm beat!" You suggest if she take a break and sharpens her saw it would go a lot faster. "I don't have time to sharpen the saw," she says. "I'm too busy sawing!"

Self-renewal activities serve to reenergize your capacities. Much like sharpening a saw, regularly engaging in self-renewal activities will make you more efficient and effective in completing your tasks and accomplishing your goals. In essence, self-renewal is the process of preserving and enhancing your greatest asset – you.

We have grown up in a world which revolves around the use and acquisition of products. For many, this results in a belief we can buy something that will either make us feel better or fix something wrong in our lives. You can turn on the television at any time and hear that, by buying a certain product you will look better, feel better, or have higher quality relationships in your life. Historically, we have affected the quality of our lives through innovations and products. Indoor pluming, refrigeration, transportation, indoor cooling and heating, and new medicines are just a few examples. Yet, today, with all these products, we have unprecedented depression, anxiety disorders, obesity, and a general loss of meaning in the lives of many people. Encouraging individuals to view excellence as a process one lives rather than a product one acquires, is fundamental to helping them get where they want to go.

Self-renewal is the process of preserving and enhancing the inner strength and core capacities needed to meet the increasing demands of your life. The renewal of core capacities mirror the idea of organismic unity, recognizing the interrelationship between the four areas from which you draw energy: physical, mental, emotional, and spiritual. For years, philosophers and practitioners have emphasized importance of renewing or reenergizing these capacities to maintain personal health and effectiveness. Regular renewal allows you to experience life more fully by increasing your capacity to stay positive, energetic, and alert for extended periods of time. The greater the intensity of your work or the greater the stress you experience, the more energy you expend and the more you draw from these sources. Therefore, you must renew these capacities if you are to continue to work or perform at a high level.

Physical Renewal

Although expending physical energy is just one way you stress your system, your physical capacity is perhaps the most import energy source to renew. When you are physically fatigued it is difficult to muster the necessary energy to focus properly or perform even simple physical tasks. Physical renewal is commonly associated with sensations of restoration, reduced muscle tension, and fatigue. Self-renewal of your physical capacity involves: eating correctly, exercising on a regular basis, and getting sufficient rest and relaxation.

Sleep: Without a doubt, sleep is your most important renewal activity. Although, the precise amount of sleep you need depends on a number of factors, there is consensus among experts that 7 to 8 hours of sleep is required for optimal functioning in high pressure environments. Sleep-deprived individuals suffer considerably more fatigue and average twice as many infectious incidents. Developing a structured sleep ritual where you go to bed at the same time and get up at the same time, whenever possible, is a great strategy for renewing your physical capacity.

Nutrition: The timing, frequency, and content of meals are extremely important as a reenergizing function. Adequate amounts of food and water is a high priority renewal strategy. Incorporating highly specific nutritional rituals will help you manage high stress situations. From a performance perspective, one of the most important nutritional strategies is to eat many small meals throughout the day, about every 2 hours. This raises metabolic rate, stabilizes mood and energy levels. To stabilize you blood sugar level throughout the day, you should eat a nutritious breakfast, eat light meals and drink plenty of water (about eight glasses). Taking a daily multivitamin, multi-mineral supplement is recommended because, no matter how good your diet is, most people miss essential vitamins and minerals.

Exercise: Exercise is a powerful mechanism for mental, physical and emotional renewal. Exercise is a biochemical event that helps to wash away the toxic chemicals of stress. Exercise effects mood states, self-concept and your overall stress response. Some recommendations for exercise as a renewal activity include: 20 to 30 minutes of moderate intensity exercise, exposing yourself to abdominal stress since abdominal muscles are the foundation of body fitness, and training to stay flexible (allowing for better posture and fewer aches and pains).

In the exercise below, think about and write down, the activities you currently engage to renew or reenergize your physical capacity. On a scale of 1 to 10, with 10 being the highest, rate how effective you feel each of these activities are in regularly renewing your physical energy.

Physical Renewal	Current Activity	1-10
Sleep		
Nutrition		
Exercise		
Other:		

Mental Renewal

We often underestimate how much mental energy we expend during the day given our tendency to multitask and the intensity and frequency of our contact with various technologies (e.g., instant messaging, emails, and Facebook). You expend mental energy whenever you focus and refocus on a task, engage in cognitive activities (i.e., writing, reflecting, analyzing) and especially when you worry. Signals of adequate mental renewal are increased calmness, creativity, and flexibility of attentional focus. Common mental renewal activities include: enjoyable creative activities, time alone and listening to your favorite music.

Creative Activities: When you engage in enjoyable creative activities you experience a letting go of conscious control and heightened sense of connection to the present moment. Such activities provide a break from the cognitive process you engage in throughout the day and connect you to a part of yourself, and a "higher mind" that is full of surprise and enjoyment. Playing a musical instrument for enjoyment, writing creatively, cooking, gardening and drawing help to renew your mental capacities.

Time Alone: Most people do not spend enough quality time alone with their own thoughts and sense of self. Typically when I mention this to young people they cringe at the thought of spending time "unplugged" from their technology and the sense of boredom this might create. Given the nature of today's fast paced world, spending 20 minutes alone, away from interactions with others, phone calls, or emails, is necessary to re-calibrate your mind, reframe experiences, become more centered, and remain mentally on track.

Listening to Music: Listening to your favorite music is a great mental renewal and reenergizing activity. It provides distraction and a break from pressing issues during your day. Listening to music can change your mood and energy level. It is no accident that most athletes include some form of music to mentally prepare before a practice or competition. Listening to music results in biochemical changes that calm the mind and relax the body, reenergizing your mental capacity.

Reflect on the mental renewal activities you currently use to renew or reenergize your mental capacity. On a scale of 1 to 10, rate how effective you feel each of these activities are in regularly renewing your mental energy.

Mental Renewal	Current Activity	1-10
Creative		
Alone time		
Music		
Other:		

Emotional Renewal

For people who are extremely busy with work related tasks, it is not unusual to feel disconnected from necessary and meaningful relationships with important people in their lives. Spending time with family members, good friends, and enjoyable leisure activities with others will reconnect you with an important human value: shared experiences. Although some find spending time with others to be more necessary for emotional renewal than others, sharing experiences is a healthy human endeavor. It has been associated with increased positive emotion, enjoyment and feelings of self-worth.

Time with Friends: Quality of life is improved immensely when there is at least one other person to listen to our troubles and support us emotionally. Although not all individuals hold this value dear to their hearts, those that do, often feel frustrated and guilty for not spending more time with friends. If this is the case, you need to develop effective strategies for staying connected to important people in your life.

Time with Family: Finding creative ways to connect with family members often provides you with a new sense of energy and purpose.

Although family members can sometimes be draining, making time to socialize, eat together, or engage in physical activities can ground you by connecting you to your values and provide greater meaning in your life.

Leisure Activity: Active leisure can be a source of emotionally positive experiences. When engaged in a hobby or an exercise activity you enjoy, you tend to be more present focused. Going out to movie or restaurant with a friend can also recharge your emotional energy.

Consider the emotional renewal activities you currently use to renew or reenergize your emotional capacity and rate, on a scale of 1 to 10, how effective you feel each of these activities are in regularly renewing your emotional energy.

Emotional Renewal	Current Activity	1-10
Friends		
Family		
Leisure		
Other:		

Spiritual Renewal

Many performers in sport and performing arts desire a connection to something greater than themselves. Often, this is found through participating on a team, attaching greater meaning to a performance experience (peak experience), or connecting a greater purpose to artistic expression as a means of expanding a God given ability. Spiritual renewal provides you with a sense of purpose to your efforts and repairs the damage to your sense of inspiration and purpose that can accompany failure.

Journal Writing: Using a personal journal as a means of articulating thoughts, feelings and reactions provides an active means of reflecting upon the meaning of the day's events. It allows you to release barriers and burdens and enables you to focus on more spiritual issues in your life.

Meditation/prayer: Many people have experienced the reenergizing and calming effects of time spent in meditation or prayer. Choosing the type of meditation (e.g., mantra or object) may depend upon the individual and what is desired. Prayer is similar to meditation when focusing on a particular purpose: unlike meditation, prayer is engages in a relationship with and entrusts concerns or worries to a higher power.

Service to Others: Making yourself available to others and giving of your time is a fundamental aspect of connecting with a community of people. Individuals often find that serving others provides a sense of balance to both their life perspective and a sense of contribution to the world. Reflect upon the spiritual renewal activities you currently use to renew or reenergize this capacity. Rate on a scale of 1 to 10, how effective you feel each of these activities are in regularly renewing your spiritual energy and sense of connectedness with something greater than yourself.

Spiritual Renewal	Current Activity	1-10
Journal writing		
Meditation/ prayer		
Service to others		
Other:		

TIME MANAGEMENT

Getting through the day has become a primary goal for hard working people. Many working parents spend their mornings rushing to get themselves ready and their kids ready for the day before running off to their jobs to deal with the intensity of their workday. Then after work, it is back home to check homework, feed the family, and off to either a practice, lesson, or game. Once home again, they put the kids to bed, do some chores around the house, and fall in bed totally exhausted, only to wake-up the next day and start it all again. Although this "get'er done" task mentality is productive and often rewarded by our society, it takes a toll on the quality of our relationships and our ability to be at peace with our lives.

For many people, moving from task to task prevents any meaningful reflection or personal connection in their lives. Friends and coworkers often tell me, "There is just not enough hours in the day" to get done what needs to be done. For many, just the thought of doing something for themselves and leaving an urgent task undone brings an unbearable feeling of guilt. The necessity to complete the multiple tasks of the day, combined with the feelings of guilt when "urgent" tasks are left undone, provide a powerful argument for developing effective time management skills. The "get'er done" mentality can work but, if left unchecked, leads to feeling overwhelmed and out of control, and results in a general loss of meaning in ones day to day existence.

A common obstacle you may face in managing your daily activities and relationships lies in the way you view time. In her book, *Time Management from the Inside-Out*, Julie Morgenstern points out most people think of time as intangible. A physical space such as your closet, for example, is easier to organize because you can see it. Time, on the other hand, is completely invisible. Therefore, to become a more effective time manager, you must first change your perception of time and make it more tangible. In other words, just as your closet has limited space into which you must fit objects, your daily, and weekly schedule is limited and can only fit a certain number of tasks. Identifying what is important to you and giving these activities and relationships a home is at the heart of self-management.

CHECK UP FROM THE NECK UP

Julie Morgenstern suggests the following exercise to better understand your current relationship with time. Think about your daily and weekly experience and work through these questions quickly, writing brief answers in the blanks.

I. What's working?

1. No matter how busy I get, I always find time for
   _____

2. My goals are well defined when it comes to
   _____

3. I am pretty clear on how long it takes me to
   _____

4. I never procrastinate about
   _____

5. I am never late for
   _____

6. It's easy for me to say no to
   _____

7. Meeting deadlines is easiest for me when
   _____

8. I am happiest when I am
   _____

II. What's not working?

1. I never have time to
   _____

2. I spend way too much time on
   _____

3. I don't have well-defined goals for
   _____

4. One thing I wish I could do every day is
   _____

5. I always underestimate how long it takes to
   _____

6. I procrastinate whenever I have to
   _____

7. I am usually late for
   _____

8. It's hard for me to say no to
   _____

9. I have a hard time getting started on
   _____

10. I have a hard time finishing
    _____

III. What I'd like to change...

List the problem areas you are most willing to address to create positive change.

1. _____

2. _____

3. _____

What processes from the "what's working" section could be applied to these areas of change?

1. _____

2. _____

3. _____

POSITIVE TIME MANAGEMENT RITUALS

Rituals are patterns of thoughts and behaviors organized in a deliberate sequence leading to a specific goal. You probably have a morning hygiene ritual that includes washing, combing your hair, and brushing your teeth. You most likely complete this pattern of behaviors in a consistent sequence almost every morning, making it a ritual. When you were a child you may have had a very specific bedtime ritual that included a bath, putting on pajamas, brushing your teeth and a bedtime story. Positive rituals serve many purposes in both your personal life and your life as a musician. There are spiritual rituals helping us connect to a greater power and provide meaning in our personal lives. There are family rituals helping maintain a sense of community and caring among family members such as Sunday dinner or watching a favorite show on television together. As a musician, you may have a deliberate pre-practice ritual helping prepare yourself through a sequence of thoughts and behaviors designed to help you become more alert and focused before your practice session.

Negative rituals involve maladaptive thoughts and behaviors resulting in diminished mental, emotional, physical or spiritual capacities. These include using alcohol as a ritual for relaxation or eating as a ritual for stress reduction. Rituals involving drugs, alcohol, food or even excessive negative thinking (e.g., Beating yourself up), have obvious maladaptive consequences. Unlike negative rituals which often disconnect or disengage you from the present, interfere with your ability to approach situations in a focused manner, or prevent you from responding to events in ways that keep you motivated and confident; positive rituals result in greater engagement in and connectedness to your current or upcoming task.

Positive time management rituals are designed to help you prepare for your week and plan for your day. When you first arrive at your office, you may have a "morning office ritual" that helps you to plan for and review your events, tasks and meetings for that day, enhancing your preparedness for the demands of the day. Two positive time management rituals you can use to become more deliberate in accomplishing daily task, and focus on your priorities are the weekly planning ritual at the beginning of each week, preferably Sunday night, and the daily planning ritual before you begin your workday.

Weekly Planning Ritual

Your weekly planning ritual should take place at the beginning of each week as a means of organizing and prioritizing your weekly activities. This organizing and prioritizing process is completed using a week-at-a-glance style calendar. It is understood that quality processes are necessary for quality outcomes in many areas of life besides the process of managing your time. For example, a predetermined process is necessary for tasks as simple as making coffee to ones as complex as adding an addition onto a house. In all aspects of life, there are sequential activities that are necessary to achieve and sustain success. Including a weekly planning ritual into your busy life is just one more example of the sequential activities necessary to get what you want in life. Although we often understand and accept the value of process in many other areas of our lives, we sometimes overlook the sequences involved in managing time effectively. This is one of the most important processes in our lives. Organizing your weekly priorities is an important time management strategy but your ability to execute your plan is equally important. Managing yourself and your tasks throughout the week is all about making choices. Being a good time manager is the difference between someone who "talks the talk" and someone who "walks the walk."

How might you go about becoming a better manager of your time? When you think of obstacles to managing your time effectively, what do you think of? One area that might be holding you back may be technical in nature. The following are technical strategies for planing your week.

Find a Home for Each Task: To begin your weekly planning ritual, it is helpful to schedule *what* to do and *when* you will do it. Finding a "home" in your schedule for each task allows you to create time boundaries or time limits for each task. Making your activities more visible and measurable gives them a place in your schedule. By creating this place or home for your tasks during the week, you will be able to schedule time for things you *want to* do instead of spending your time doing things you *have to* do.

Estimate the Length of Each Task: Do you know how long a particular task will take? Once you become a good "task time estimator" you will be more accurate at giving tasks a home in your schedule. Take the time to record estimated and actual completion time to determine how well you estimate your task times.

Use Time Zones: There are many tasks you can "funnel" into time zones that match your energy cycles. This means you determine which tasks are best completed at certain times of the day. For example, you might find reading in the afternoon difficult due to your low energy cycle. Therefore it might be best for you to read in the mornings and answer emails in the afternoon. You should be able to put 80% of your tasks into time zones where you will be most effective and efficient.

Set a Realistic Workload for the Week: Once you get better at estimating the amount of time tasks take to complete, you will find it easier to plan a more realistic workload for each day.

Boulders, Rocks and Pebbles

How do you decide what is important to do, when to do it, and how much of it to do? Because of the over scheduled nature of your week, it becomes easy to simply do what is in front of you or complete what is most urgent at the time. When organizing your week, first think of the parts of your weekly schedule that are non-moveable. These can be considered *boulders* (i.e., things like class times, practice times and appointments that you cannot change). At the beginning of each week, fill the boulders in first. Next fill in the *rocks*. These are activities you want to keep in your day but can move if you have to. For example, lunch, renewal activities, or study times are rocks. Finally, include the *pebbles* in your week. These are things you can move from day to day but would like to complete that week. For example, specific times for making phone calls, retuning emails or activities you enjoy but can move if necessary.

Weekly Roles and Goals

Creating effective balance between the roles you play in your life and the goals you have for yourself can be a daunting task. It may seem impossible but you can get closer to creating balance in your week by understanding what it is you are trying to balance. Everyone divides their life roles or categories differently. Understanding the roles you have in your life and developing weekly goals for each role goes a long way to help you execute around your priorities and achieve a greater sense of balance in your life. Some examples of life roles include: parent, spouse, student, friend, church member and musician.

During your weekly preparation ritual, write in your important life roles in your week-at-a-glance schedule (example below). Identify the goals you want to accomplish in that role during the week. For example, in my role as a parent, my weekly goals might be: 1. Drop off and pick up my son from school on Monday, Wednesday and Friday (these would be a boulders), 2. Help with homework two nights, Tuesday and Thursday (these would be rocks because I could trade nights if necessary), 3. Attend tennis match on Saturday (A boulder) and 4. Go to dinner with the tennis team after match (This would be a pebble, depending on my son's wishes).

Week of:	Monday	Tuesday	Wednesday	Thursday	Friday	Saturday
Role Goals:	7 Ian School	7	7 Ian School	7	7 Ian School	
	8	8	8	8	8	Ian Tennis
	9	9	9	9	9	
	10	10	10	10	10	Tennis Dinner
	11	11	11	11	11	
	12	12	12	12	12	
	1	1	1	1	1	Sunday
	2	2	2	2	2	
	3	3	3	3	3	
	4	4	4	4	4	
	5	5	5	5	5	
	Evening	Evening Ian Homework	Evening	Evening Ian Homework	Evening	

Daily Planning Ritual

How do you prepare yourself to begin your day? Taking ten to fifteen minutes at the beginning of each day to formulate a plan will help you to get mentally organized and emotionally ready to execute your daily plan. In today's fast paced world we often over look the importance of our morning time and the role it plays in setting the tone for the rest of the day. If your morning time feels like a "fire drill" where you are rushing around the house with barely enough time to make it out the door, you are starting your day in a stressed or agitated way. Implementing a morning planning ritual allows you to formulate your plan for that day. This helps you to begin the day calmly and with a since of purpose and preparation. Your daily planning ritual is a great time for prayer, meditation or quite time. This harnesses your resources and prepares you for the rest of your day.

To execute your daily plan effectively you may find it helpful to use a time quadrant system that groups tasks based on time estimated to complete and simplifies complex or more time consuming tasks by breaking them up into smaller, more manageable parts. Using the quadrant system, you can group tasks that are similar in time category, such as, quick tasks (e.g., tasks that take less than five minutes each, emails and phone calls) and intermediate tasks (e.g., Tasks that take 15-30 minutes to complete, drop off dry cleaning, eat lunch, check mail box). You may want to include a quadrant dealing with longer term tasks or projects. This quadrant allows you to keep track of the smaller tasks needed to complete each project. The fourth quadrant can be used in many different ways. For example, you can record tasks that have come up during the day but do not need to be completed until later that week or simple at-a-glance reminders for you to use to check periodically. Below is an example of a daily quadrant system for a golf professional.

Quick Tasks	Intermediate Tasks
Calls and Emails 1. Mr. Jones – return call 2. Mr. Smith – Saturday apt. 3. Mrs. White – clinic 4. Callaway order	**Tasks and Errands** 1. Create flier 2. Develop lesson plan 3. Grade homework
Projects	Reminders
Golf Tournament 1. Make list of possible families 2. Check hotel availability & rates 3. Maps and contact information	1. Afternoon workout 2. Evening practice session 3. Pick up milk on way home

GOAL ATTAINMENT

Goal attainment strategies are some of the most researched topics in sport and performance psychology. Setting practice goals has been shown to influence performance across a variety of tasks, skill levels, and age groups. Having goals or targets to shoot for during a practice session direct your attentional focus to important aspects of performance and mobilize your effort to hit your targets. This increases your persistence to overcome obstacles.

Continuing to develop as a musician requires you to identify short-term or weekly practice goals for various musical aspects important to your performance. These goals act as daily targets that direct your attention and effort during practice while moving you closer to your long-term performance goal. Although not everyone has the same goals, most musicians have similar developmental categories. The steps in your goal attainment process involve: Identifying your key performance categories and intermediate goals (6-month goals), developing training activities for each performance goal, and planning your practice week.

Identify Key Performance Categories and Goals

Write down your major performance categories and what you would like to achieve over the next six months in each. Performance categories might include: mental, technical, musical and physical. When you write down your goals for each of your performance categories, think about what you want *to be* like in 6-months.

Performance Category	What I want to be like in the next 6-months

Develop Practice Goals and Training Activities

Once you have identified your key performance activities and intermediate goals, review your intermediate goals and develop short-term practice goals. For example, if "Trusting what I've trained" is a 6-month mental goal for a specific performance piece, then mental practice goals might include: increase acceptance of mistakes, develop my concentration muscle, and commit to training

trust. Some training activities used to accomplish these goals might be:
1. Keep a mental practice journal
2. Practice focus drills
3. Use variable practice every practice session.

Some of the most common problems people face when developing practice goals and training activities are setting too many goals too soon and setting goals that are too general. When developing your goals, spend time prioritizing them based on the most meaningful. Strive to accomplish one or two at a time. Additionally, your goals and training activities need to be specific. Take some time to reflect on your 6-month goals and develop practice goals and training activities for each using the table on the next page.

Practice Goals	Training Activities
Mental Goals	
1. _____	
2. _____	
3. _____	
Technical Goals	
1. _____	
2. _____	
3. _____	
Musical Goals	
1. _____	
2. _____	
3. _____	
Physical Goals	
1. _____	
2. _____	
3. _____	

Plan Your Practice Week

Perhaps the most important goal attainment strategy is planning your practice week. Much has been written on the benefits of deliberate practice and committing to a thoughtful plan. This is an essential aspect of a deliberate, focused practice session. Keep in mind that being flexible in your goals is necessary if your progress is interrupted or your goals are unrealistic. Once you set your goals and plan your practice week, make a full commitment to following your plan but be flexible to making adjustments in your goals when needed.

Using the form below, think through this upcoming week and develop a practice plan. You may also choose to include specific renewal activities for certain days of the week.

	Plan for Week 1	
Day	Practice / Performance Activities	Renewal
MONDAY	1. 2. 3.	
TUESDAY	1. 2. 3.	
WEDNESDAY	1. 2. 3.	
THURSDAY	1. 2. 3.	
FRIDAY	1. 2. 3.	
SATURDAY/ SUNDAY	1. 2. 3.	

POSTSCRIPT

To reach a lofty goal, you will need to sacrifice short-term gains for long-term progress. In other words, you will need to put-off or delay something gratifying to put-in the time needed to achieve your goal. You may be required to practice early in the morning to get studio time; sacrificing sleep, morning time with your family, or evening time because you must go to bed early to awake rested and ready to practice.

As the speed of the world around us increases, we develop a mentality that things in our lives can be fixed quickly and with little effort. Evidence of quick-fix solutions is seen at many levels in our society. In sports, education, relationships, personal health, and business practices, many individuals attempt to sacrifice long-term gains for short-term rewards. Many people look to change the way they think, eat, or cope, trying to tough it out: they may think these solutions will get them over the hump. Although quick fixes contain pieces of the solution; ultimately, they produce short-term results at best. Thinking positively, losing weight to help self-image, and gaining control over negative feelings may be beneficial, but they are simply pieces of a larger, more comprehensive puzzle. Making it happen for you as a musician is grounded in your self-management skills. Your ability to manage your time, renew your energy and attain your goals work together to get where you want to go and help you play your best when it counts.

SELF-REFLECTION QUESTIONS

1. As a musician there are a number of different mental aspects making up your total performance. For each mental aspect below, project yourself forward in time and write a brief statement of how you would most like to be described in that particular performance aspect.

Mental skill	How I would like to be described
Trust	
Confidence	
Concentration	
Composure	
Commitment	

1. Once you have identified your major life categories, you can begin the process of determining what you want to achieve in each. In the exercise below, identify five major roles or categories in your life and include goals you have for each category.

Life Category	Goals

Notes

Notes

Resources

Playing Your Best Workbook

In today's high pressure performance environments, a thoughtful and integrated approach to the development and refinement of mental performance skills is necessary. This workbook is designed to provide a solid foundation for developing and executing mental performance skills necessary for playing your best when it counts

Playing Your Best Journal

Whether you are a professional musician or simply passionate about performing music, when you are mentally stronger you are able to practice and perform with more energy, passion, and purpose. This journal will help you play your best while helping you become more strength-focused and solution-oriented during practices.

Playing Your Best Seminars, workshops and presentations

Seminars, workshops and presentations are designed to meet the specific needs of each group whether presenting at music events, professional conferences, or organizational and university settings. Presentations typically last from one to two hours whiles seminars may be conducted over the course of one or two days.

QUICK ORDER FORM

On-line orders: www.playingyourbest.com

Telephone orders: Call 405.361.4474

Email orders: Bill@playingyourbest.com

For seminars and workshops
Contact Dr. Moore
Bill@playingyourbest.com
Call (405) 361.4474

For information on other books for musicians
Written by Dr. Moore
Visit www.playingyourbest.com

TO ORDER THIS BOOK ON-LINE
Go to: www.Playingyourbest.com

MOORE PERFORMANCE CONSULTING PUBLICATION